HOME-MAKING

HOME-MAKING

WHAT THE BIBLE SAYS ABOUT ROLES AND RELATIONSHIPS IN A HARMONIOUS CHRISTIAN HOUSEHOLD

REV. J.R. MILLER, D.D.

THE VISION FORUM, INC.
SAN ANTONIO, TEXAS

Originally Published in 1882

Fourth Printing
Copyright © 2003 The Vision Forum, Inc.
All Rights Reserved

"Where there is no vision, the people perish."

The Vision Forum, Inc.
4719 Blanco Rd., San Antonio, Texas 78212
www.visionforum.com

ISBN: 1-929241-35-6

Typography by Jeremy M. Fisher
Cover Design by Joshua R. Goforth

Printed in the United States of America

CONTENTS

INTRODUCTORY

This book is written in the hope that its pages may carry inspiration and a little help, perhaps, to those who desire to do faithful work for God within their own doors. Its aim is to mark out the duties and responsibilites of each member of the household, and to suggest how each may do a part in making the home-life what God meant it to be.

THE WEDDED LIFE

The benediction that falls upon the homes of a country is like the gentle rain that descends among the hills. A thousand springs are fuller afterward, and along the banks of a thousand streamlets flowing through the valleys the grass is greener and the flowers pour out richer fragrance.

Homes are the springs among the hills, whose many streamlets, uniting, form like great rivers society, the community, the nation, the Church. If the springs run low the rivers waste; if they pour out bounteous currents the rivers are full. If the springs are pure the rivers are clear like crystal; if they are foul the rivers are defiled. A curse upon homes sends a poisoning blight everywhere; a blessing sends healing and new life into every channel.

Homes are the divinely ordained fountains of life. It is not by accident that men live in families rather than solitarily. The human race began in a family, and Eden was a home. The divine blessing has ever rested upon nations and communities just in the measure in which they have added to these original institutions and have kept marriage and the home pure and holy; and blight and curse have come just in the measure in which they have departed from these divine models, dishonoring marriage and tearing down the sacred walls of home.

Back of the home lies marriage. The wedding day throws its shadow far down the future; it may be, ought to be, a shadow of healing and benediction.

In a tale of medieval English life a maiden goes before the bridal party on their way to the church, strewing flowers in their path. This was meant to signify that their wedded life should be one of joy and prosperity. Almost universally, wedding ceremonies and festivities have some feature of similar significance, implying that the occasion is one of gladness. In some countries flowers are worn as bridal wreaths. In some they are woven into garlands for the waist, the tying of the ends being a part of the ritual. In others they are carried in the hand or worn in the hair or on the bosom. Music comes in also, always joyous music, implying that the ceremony is one of peculiar gladness. In some places, too, wedding bells are rung, their peals being merry and gladsome.

All these and similar bridal customs indicate that the world regards the wedding as the crowning day of life, and marriage as an event of the highest felicity, an occasion for the most enthusiastic congratulations. Yet not always are these happy prophecies fulfilled. Sometimes the flowers wither and the music grows discordant and the wedding peals die away into a memory only of gladness. It ought not to be so. It is not so when the marriage has been true, and when the wedded life is ruled by love. Then the bridal wreath remains fresh and fragrant till it is laid upon the coffin by the loving hands of the one who survives to close the eyes of the other; and the wedding music and the peals of the bells continue to echo in tones of gladness and peace until hushed in the sobbings of sorrow when the singers sing in dirges and the bells toll out the number of the finished years.

Marriage is intended to bring joy. The married life is meant to be the happiest, fullest, purest, richest life. It is God's own ideal of completeness. It was when He saw that it was not good for man to be alone that woman was made and brought to him to supply what was lacking. The divine intention, therefore, is that marriage shall yield happiness and that it shall add to the fullness of the life of both husband and wife; that neither shall lose, but that both shall gain. If in any use it fails to be a blessing and to yield joy, and a richer, fuller life, the fault cannot be with the institution itself, but with those who, under its shadow, fail to fulfill its conditions.

The causes of failure may lie back of the marriage altar, for many are united in matrimony who never should have entered upon such a union; or they may lie in the life after marriage, for many who might attain to the very highest happiness in wedded life, fail to do so because they have not learned the secret of living happily together.

To guard against the former mistake, the sacred character and the solemn responsibilities of marriage should be well understood and thoughtfully considered by all who would enter upon it. Marriage is a divine ordinance. It was part of God's original intention when he made man. It is not a mere human arrangement, something that sprang up in the race as a convenience along the history of the ages. It was not devised by any earthly lawgiver. It is not a habit into which men fell in the early days. The stamp of divine intention and ordination is upon it.

As a relationship, it is the closest and most sacred on earth. The relation of parent and child is very close. Children are taught in all the Scriptures to honor their parents, to revere them, to cleave to them, to brighten and bless their lives in every possible way. Yet the marriage relation is put above the filial, for a man is to leave his father and his mother, give up his old home with all its sacred ties and memories, and cleave to his wife. After marriage a husband's first and highest duties are to his wife, and a wife's to her husband. The two are to live for each other. Life is to be lost for life. Every other interest is thenceforward secondary to the home interest.

Then the marriage relation is indissoluble. The two

become in the fullest, truest sense one. Each is incomplete
before; marriage is the uniting of two halves in one
complete whole. It is the knitting together of two lives in a
union so close and real that they are no more twain, but
one; so close that nothing save death or the one crime of
infidelity to the marriage bond itself can disunite them.
Marriage, therefore, is not a contract which can be annulled
at the will of one or both of the parties. It may be
discovered after the marriage has been formed that the
parties are ill mated; one may find in the other traits or
habits unsuspected before which seem to render happiness
in union impossible; the husband may be cruel and abusive
or the wife ill-tempered, thriftless or a burden; yet the
Scriptures are very explicit in their teaching that the tie
once formed is indissoluble. There is one crime, said the
pure and holy Jesus, which, committed by either, leaves the
guilty one as dead, the other free. But besides this the
teachings of Christ recognize no other lawful sundering of
the marriage tie. When two persons stand at the marriage
altar and with clasped hands promise before God and in the
presence of human witnesses to take each other as wife and
as husband, to keep and to cherish each the other, only
death can unclasp their hands. Each takes into sacred
keeping the happiness and the highest good of the other to
the end of life.

In view of the sacredness and indissolubleness of this

relation and the many tender and far-reaching interests that
inhere in it, it is but the simplest commonplace to say that
the greatest care should be taken before marriage to make
sure that the union will be a true one, that the two lives will
sweetly blend together, and that each will be able to make
the other at least measurably happy. Yet obvious as is the
fact, nonetheless it is profoundly important that it should
be heeded. If there were more wise and honest forethought
with regard to marriage, there would be less after-thought
of regret and repenting.

A word may fitly be spoken here concerning the
marriage formalities. The wedding day is one that should
ever be remembered and held sacred among life's
anniversaries. It is the day whose benediction should fall on
all other days to the end of life. It should stand out in the
calendar bright with all the brightness of love and gratitude.
The memory of the wedding-hour in a happy married life
should shine like a star, even in old age. It is surely worthwhile, therefore, to make the occasion itself just as
delightful as possible, to gather about it and into it whatever
will help to make it memorable, so that it shall stand out
bright and sacred among all life's days and hours. This is
not done when the marriage is secret; there are no
associations about the event in that case to make its
memory a source of pleasure in after years. Nor is it done
when, on the other hand, the occasion is made one of great

levity or of revelry; the joy of marriage is not hilarious, but deep and quiet.

On the wedding-day the happy pair should have about them their true friends, those whom they desire to hold in close relations in their after life. It is no time for insincerity; it is no place for empty professions of friendship. Everything about the circumstances, the festivities, the formalities, the marriage ceremony itself, the congratulations, should be so ordered as to cause no jar, no confusion, nothing to mar the perfect pleasure of the occasion, and so as to leave only the pleasantest memory behind. These may seem too insignificant matters for mention here, yet it is surely worth-while to make the occasion of one's wedding such that it shall always be remembered with a thrill of delight, with only happy associations and without one smallest incident or feature to mar the perfectness of its memory.

But it is when the wedding ceremony is over, and the two are one, that the life begins which has so many possibilities of happiness, of growth, of nobleness of character, of heroism in living, of tender romance in loving. Angels hover about the marriage altar and hush their songs while hands are clasped and holy vows are plighted and then spread their sheltering wings over the happy pair as they start out together on the voyage of life. The greatest blessedness, the highest development of character, the noblest manhood and womanhood, the most perfect attainments in Christian life, are to be reached in the marriage relation, if it is made what God meant it to be. It will be the fault of those who wed, of one or of both, if marriage proves aught but a blessing, and if the happiness of either is wrecked in the voyage together.

Yet it must not be concluded that the bridal gate opens essentially into a garden of Eden. Marriage is not the panacea for all life's ills. It does not of itself lead invariably and necessarily to all that is noble and beautiful in life. While its possibilities of happiness and blessing are so great, its possibility of failure must not be ignored. Only a true and wise—only the truest and wisest—wedded life will realize the blessings of the ideal marriage relation.

The first lesson to be learned and practiced is loving *patience*. It requires some time to bring any two lives into perfect unison, so that they shall blend in every chord and tone. No matter how intimate the relations may have been before, neither knows much of the real life of the other until they meet with every separating wall and every thinnest veil removed.

In China the bridegroom does not see his bride until she is brought to him on his wedding-day closely veiled and locked up in a sedan chair. The key is handed to him when the chair reaches his house, and he unlocks the door, lifts the veil and takes his first look at his treasure. Brides and bridegrooms with us are not usually such strangers to each other as among the "Celestials;" they see each other's face often enough, but it is doubtful whether as a rule they really know much more of each other's inner life. Even without any intention to hide their true selves or to appear veiled, it is only after marriage that their acquaintanceship becomes complete. There are graces of character and disposition that are then discovered for the first time; and there are also faults, peculiarities of habit, of taste, of temper, never suspected before, which then disclose themselves.

It is just at this point that one of the greatest perils of wedded life is met. Some are disappointed and discouraged by the discovery of these points of uncongeniality, these possibilities of discord, concluding at once that their marriage was a mistake and must necessarily be a failure. Their beautiful dream is shattered and they make no effort to build it again. But really all that is needed is wise and loving patience. There is no reason for discouragement much less for despair. It is entirely possible, notwithstanding the discovery of these points of friction and uncongeniality, to realize the highest ideal of wedded life. It is like the meeting of two rivers. At first there is confusion, excitement, commotion, and apparent conflict and strife as the two flow together and it seems as if they never would blend and comingle; but in little time they unite in one broad peaceful stream, rolling in majesty and strength, without a trace of strife. So when two independent lives, with diverse habits, tastes and peculiarities first meet, to be united in one, there is embarrassment, there is perplexity, there is seeming conflict, there is the dashing of life against life at many points. Sometimes it may seem as if they never could blend in one and as if the conflict must go on hopelessly for ever; but with loving patience the two will in due time coalesce and unite in one life—nobler, stronger, fuller, deeper, richer—and move on in calmness and peace.

Perfect harmony cannot be forced in a day—cannot indeed be forced at all—but must come through gentleness and perhaps only after many days. There must be mutual adaptation, and time must be allowed for this. The present duty is unselfish love. Each must forget self in devotion to the other. Each must blame self and not the other when anything goes wrong. There must be the largest and gentlest forbearance. Impatience may wreck all. A sharp word may retard for months the process of soul-blending. There must be the determination on the part of both to make the marriage happy and to conquer everything that lies in the way. Then the very differences between the two lives will become their closest points of union. When they have passed through the process of blending, though it may for the time be painful and perilous, the result will be a wedded life of deep peace, quiet joy and inseparable affection.

Another secret of happiness in married life is *courtesy*. By what law of nature or of life is it that after the peals of the wedding bells have died away, and they have established themselves in their own home, so many husbands and wives drop the charming little amenities and refinements or manner toward each other that so invariably and delightfully characterized their intercourse before marriage? Is there no necessity for these civilities any longer? Are they so sure now of each other's love that they do not need to give expression to it, either in affectionate word or act? Is wedded love such a strong, vigorous and self-sufficing entity that it never needs sunshine, rain or dew? Is politeness merely a manner that is necessary in intercourse with the outside world, and not required when we are alone with those we love the best? Are hearts so peculiarly constituted that they are not pained or offended by things that would never be pardoned in us if done in ordinary society? Are we under no obligations to be respectful and to pay homage to our dearest friends, while even to the rudest clown or the veriest stranger we meet outside our own doors we feel ourselves bound to show the most perfect civility?

On the contrary, there is no place in the world where the amenities of courtesy should be so carefully maintained as in the home. There are no hearts that hunger so for expressions of affection as the hearts of which we are most sure. There is no love that so needs its daily bread as the love that is strongest and holiest. There is no place where rudeness or incivility is so unpardonable as inside our own doors and toward our best beloved. The tenderer the love and the truer, the more it craves the thousand little attentions and kindnesses which so satisfy the heart. It is not costly presents at Christmas and on birthdays and anniversaries that are wanted; these are only mockeries if the days between are empty of affectionate expressions. Jewelry and silks and richly-bound volumes will never atone for the want of warmth and tenderness. Between husband and wife there should be maintained without break or pause, the most perfect courtesy, the gentlest attention, the most unselfish amiability, the utmost affectionateness. Coleridge says: "The happiness of life is made up of minute fractions, the little soon-forgotten charities of a kiss or a smile, a kind look, a heartfelt compliment, and the countless infinitesimals of pleasurable thought and genial feeling." These may seem trifles, and the omission of them may be deemed unworthy of thought; but they are the daily bread of love, and hearts go hungry when they are omitted. It may be only carelessness at first in a busy husband or a weary wife that fails in these small, sweet courtesies, and it may seem a little matter, but in the end the result may be a growing far apart of two lives which might have been for ever very happy in each other had their early love but been cherished and nourished.

"For love will starve if it is not fed,
And true hearts pray for their daily bread."

Another important element in married life is *unity of interest*. There is danger that wedded lives drift apart because their employments are nearly always different. The husband is absorbed in business, in his profession, in severe daily toil; the wife has her home duties, her social life, her friends and friendships, her children; and the two touch at no point. Unless care is taken this separation of duties and engagements will lead to actual separation in heart and life. To prevent this each should keep up a constant loving interest in whatever the other does. The husband may listen every evening to the story of the home-life of the day, its incidents, its pleasures, its perplexities, its trials, the children's sayings and doings, what the neighbors said who dropped in, the bits of news that have been heard, and may enter with zest and sympathy into everything that is told him. Nothing that concerns the wife of his heart should be too small for even the gigantic intellect of the greatest of husbands. In personal biography few things are more charming and fascinating than the glimpses into the homes of some of the greatest men of earth, when we see them, having laid aside the cares and honors of the world, enter their own doors to romp with the children, to listen to their prattle, and to talk over with loving interest all the events and incidents of the day's home-history.

In like manner, every wise and true-hearted wife will desire to keep up an interest in all her husband's affairs. She will want to know of every burden, every struggle, every plan, every new ambition. She will wish to learn what undertaking has succeeded and what has failed, and to keep herself thoroughly familiar and in full sympathy with all his daily, personal life.

No marriage is complete which does not unite and blend the wedded lives at every point. This can be secured only by making every interest common to both. Let both hearts throb with the same joy and share each pang of sorrow. Let the same burdens rest on the shoulders of both. Let the whole life be made common.

In another sense still should their lives blend. They should read and study together, having the same line of thought, helping each other toward a higher mental culture. They should worship together, praying side by side, communing on the holiest themes of life and hope, and together carrying to God's feet the burdens of their hearts for their children and for every precious object. Why should they not talk together of their personal trials, their peculiar temptations, their infirmities, and help each other by sympathy, by brave word and by intercession, to be victorious in living?

Thus they should live one life as it were, not two.

Every plan and hope of each should embrace the other. The moment a man begins to leave his wife out of any part of his life, or that she has plans, hopes, pleasures, friendships or experiences from which she excludes him, there is peril in the home. They should have no secrets which they keep from each other. They should have no companions or friends save those which they have in common. Thus their two lives should blend in one life, with no thought, no desire, no feeling, no joy or sorrow, no pleasure or pain unshared.

Into the inner sanctuary of this wedded life no third party should ever be admitted. In its derivation the word home contains the idea of seclusion. It shuts its inmates away from all the other life of the world about them. I have read of a young wife who prepared one little room in her house into which none but herself and her husband were ever to enter. The incident is suggestive. Even in the sanctuary of the home-life there should be an inner holy of holies, open only to husband and wife, into which no other eye ever shall peer, in which no other voice ever shall be heard to speak. No stranger should ever intermeddle with this holy life, no confidential friend should ever hear confidences from this inner sanctuary. No window or door should ever be opened into it, and no report should ever be carried out of what goes on within. The blended life they twain are living should be between themselves and God only.

Another rule for wedded life is to watch against every

smallest beginning of misunderstanding or alienation. In the wreck of many a home there lingers still the memory of months or years of very tender wedded life. The fatal estrangement that rent the home asunder and made scandal for the world began in a little difference which a wise, patient word might have composed. But the word was not spoken—an unwise, impatient word was spoken instead—and the trivial breach remained unclosed, and grew wider till two hearts that had been knit together as one were torn for ever apart. Rarely are estrangements the work of one day, or caused by one offence; they are growths.

> "It is the little rift within the lute
> That by and by will make the music mute,
> And, ever-widening, slowly silence all—
> The little rift within the lover's lute:
> Or little Pitted speck in garnered fruit,
> That, rotting inward, slowly moulders all."

It is against the beginnings of alienations, therefore, that sacred watch must be kept. Has a hasty word been spoken? Instantly recall it and ask for forgiveness. Is there a misunderstanding? No matter whose the fault may be, do not allow it to remain one hour. Is the home-life losing a little of its warmth? Ask not for the cause nor where the blame lies, but hasten to get back the old fervor at any cost.

Never allow a second word to be spoken in a quarrel. Let not the sun go down upon an angry thought or feeling between two hearts that have been united as one. Pride must have no place in wedded life. There must never be any standing upon dignity, nor any nice calculation as to whose place it is to make the apology or to yield first to the other. True love knows no such casualty; it seeks not its own; it delights in being foremost in forgiving and yielding. There is no lesson that husbands and wives need more to learn than instantly and always to seek forgiveness of each other whenever they are conscious of having in any way caused pain or committed a wrong. The pride that will never say, "I did wrong; forgive me," is not ready for wedded life.

> "Oh, we do all offend—
> There's not a day of wedded life, if we
> Count at its close the little, bitter sum
> Of thoughts, and words, and looks unkind
>   and forward—
> Silence that chides, and woundings of the eye—
> But, prostrate at each other's feet, we should
> Each night forgiveness ask."

A writer closes a book on home-life with this earnest word: "The great care should be so as to live in the home that when it shall any way be lost there may be no accompanying sting of memory harder to bear than any will of God. A little constant thought, self-denial, fidelity, a true life each with each and each with God, will not only save all unavailing regret and ensure the purest peace under all experience, but make the thought of reunion and life again in the Home of God chief among incentives to his service." The only way to ensure a memory without a pang when the separating hand has done its work is to wake each hour of wedded life, as it comes, tender and true as two loving hearts can make it.

To crown all, the presence of Christ should be sought at the marriage festivity and his blessing on every day of wedded life. A lady was printing on a blackboard a text for her little girl. The text was: "Christ Jesus came into the world to save sinners." Just as she had finished it, the child entered the room and began to spell out the words. Presently she exclaimed, "Oh, mamma you have left out Jesus!" True enough, she had left out the sacred name in transcribing the verse. It is a sad omission when, in setting up their home any husband and wife leave out Jesus. No other omission they could possibly make would cause so great a want in the household. Without his presence to bless the marriage, the congratulations and good wishes of friends will be only empty words. Without his benediction on the wedded life day by day, even the fullest, richest tenderness of true affection will fail to give all that is needed to satisfy hungry hearts. Without the divine blessing, all the beauty, the gladness, the treasure which earth can give to a home will not bring peace that may not at any moment be broken.

Surely too much is involved, too great a responsibility, too many and too precious interests, to venture upon wedded life without Christ. The lessons are too hard to learn to be attempted without a divine Teacher. The burdens are too heavy to be borne without a mighty Helper. The perils of the way are too many to be passed through without an unerring Guide. The duties are too delicate, and the consequences of failure in them too far-reaching and too terrible, to be taken up without wisdom and help from above.

The prayer of the Breton mariner as he puts out on the waves is a fit prayer for every wedded life as its bark is launched: "Keep me, O God, for my boat is so small and the ocean is so wide."

THE HUSBAND'S PART

In home-making each member of the family has a part, and the fullest happiness and blessedness of the home can be attained only when each one's part is faithfully fulfilled. If any one member of the family fails in love or duty, the failure mars the whole household life, just as one discordant voice in a company of singers spoils the music, though all the others sing in perfect accord.

One person cannot alone make a home what it ought to be, what it might be. One sweet spirit may spread through the home the odors of love, even though among the other members there are bitterness and strife, just as one fragrant flower may spread through a hedge of thorns a breath of perfume. The influence of one gentle and unselfish life may also in time soften rudeness and melt selfishness, and pervade the home-life with the blessedness of love. Yet still it is true that no one member of a household can make the household life full and complete. Each must do a part. The husband has a part, all his own, which no other one can do; the wife has a part; the children, the brothers, the sisters—each has his own part. Just as the different parts in music combine to produce harmony that pleases the ear, or as the artist's colors combine on his canvas to please the eye, or as the different parts of a machine work together to produce some effect of power, of motion, of delicacy of skill; so when each member of the family is faithful in every duty and responsibility the result will be harmony, joy and blessedness.

What is the husband's part? How does the word of God define his duties as a husband? What is involved in his part of the marriage relation? What does he owe to his wife? When he stands at the marriage altar and takes the hand of his bride in his and makes solemn vows and pledges in the presence of God and of human witnesses, what is it that he engages to do?

There is one word that covers all—the word *love*. "Husbands, love your wives," comes the command, with all divine authority, from the Holy Scriptures. The counsel is very short, but it grows exceedingly long when it is fully accepted and observed.

The art of the photographer is now so perfect that he can take the whole face of a great city newspaper on a plate small enough to be worn in a little pin; yet as you look at it under the microscope you find that every word is there, every point and mark. So in this word "love" we have a whole volume of thoughts and suggestions of life and duty crowded; and as we study it closely and carefully every one of them appears distinctly and clearly written out. What are some of the things that are embraced in a husband's love?

One is *fondness, affectionate regard*. When a man offers his hand in marriage to a woman he says by his act that his heart has made choice of her among all women, that he has for her a deeper and tenderer affection than for any other. At the marriage altar he solemnly pledges to her a continuance of that love until death. When the beauty has faded from her face and the lustre from her eyes, when old age has brought wrinkles, or when sickness, care or sorrow has left marks of wasting or marring, the faithful husband's love is to remain deep and true as ever. His heart is still to choose his wife among all women and to find its truest delight in her.

But the word implies more than mere emotional fondness. The Scriptures give the measure of the love which husbands are to bear to their wives: "Husbands, love your wives, even as Christ also loved the Church and gave himself for it." There is no earthly line long enough to fathom the depths of Christ's love for his Church, and no mortal can love in the same degree; yet in so far as that love can be repeated on earth every husband is required to repeat it. Christ gave himself for his Church; the husband is to give himself, to deny himself, utterly to forget himself, in simple and wholehearted devotion to his wife. In the true husband who realizes all that this divine command involves, selfishness dies at the marriage altar. He thinks no longer of his own comfort, but of his wife's. He takes the storm himself and shelters her from its blast. He toils to support her. He denies himself that he may bring new pleasures and comforts to her. He counts no sacrifice too great to be made which will bring benefit to her.

There is something very sacred and almost awe-inspiring in the act by which a wife, at her entrance into the marriage state, confides all the interests of her life to the hands of him whom she accepts as her husband. She leaves father and mother and the home of her childhood. She severs all the ties that bound her to her old life. She gives up the friends and the friendships of her youth. She cuts herself off from the sources of happiness to which she has been accustomed to turn. She looks up into the face of him who has asked her to be his wife, and with trembling heart yet with quiet confidence she entrusts to him and to his keeping all the sacred interests of her life. It is a holy trust which he receives when she thus commits herself to his hands. It is the lifelong happiness of a tender human heart capable of ineffable joy or unmeasured misery. It is the whole future well-being of a life which may be fashioned into the image of Christ, or marred and its beauty shattered for ever.

"I wonder did you ever count
The value of one human fate,
Or scan the infinite amount
Of one heart's treasures, and the weight
Of life's one venture, and the whole
Concentrate purpose of a soul?"

The wife yields all up to the husband, gives herself in the fullest, completest sense. Will he be faithful to the holy trust reposed in his hands? Will he love her with an undecaying love? Will he shelter her from the blast and protect her in the day of peril? Will he cherish her happiness as a precious jewel, bearing all things, enduring all things, for her sake? Will he seek her highest good, help her to build up in herself the noblest womanhood? Is he worthy to receive into his keeping all that her confiding love lays at his feet? Will he be true to his trust for ever?

Miss Procter has put these words into the lips of an expectant bride—"A Woman's Question:"

"Before I trust my fate to thee,
Or place my hand in thine;
Before I let thy future give
Color and form to mine;
Before I peril all for thee,
Question thy soul to-night for me.

"I break all slighter bonds, nor feel
A shadow of regret;
Is there one link within the past
That holds thy spirit yet?
Or is thy faith as clear and free
As that which I can pledge to thee?

"Does there within thy dimmest dreams
A possible future shine,
Wherein thy life could henceforth breathe,
Untouched, unshared by mine?
If so, at any pain or cost,
Oh, tell me before all is lost.

"Look deeper still. If thou canst feel
Within thy inmost soul
That thou hast kept a portion back,
While I have staked the whole,
Let no false pity spare the blow,
But in true mercy tell me so.

"Is there within thy heart a need
That mine cannot fulfill?
One chord that any other hand
Could better wake or still?

Speak now—lest at some future day
My whole life wither and decay.

"Lives there within thy nature bid
The demon-spirit Change,
Shedding a passing glory still
On all things new and strange?—
It may not be thy fault alone—
But shield my heart against thine own.

"Couldst thou withdraw thy hand one day
And answer to my claim
That Fate, and that to-day's mistake—
Not thou—had been to blame?
Some soothe their conscience thus; but thou
Wilt surely warn and save me now."

It is a solemn thing for any man to assume such a trust and take a life—a gentle, delicate, confiding young life—into his keeping, to cherish, to shelter, to bless, until death either takes the trust out of his hands or strikes him down.

Alas how many never realize the sacredness of the responsibility they so lightly assume! How many fail, too, to keep the holy trust! How many trample with rude feet upon the delicate lives they swore at the altar to defend and cherish till death! How many let selfishness rule instead of

love! How many fail to answer the needs of the tender
hearts they have pledged themselves to fill and satisfy with
love! Every husband should understand that when a
woman, the woman of his own free and deliberate choice,
places her hand in his and thus becomes his wife, she has
taken her life, with all its hopes and fears, all its possibilities
of joy or sorrow, all its capacity for development, all its
tender and sacred interests, and placed it in his hand, and
that he is under the most solemn obligations to do all in his
power to make that life happy, beautiful, noble and blessed.
To do this he must be ready to make any personal sacrifice.
Nothing less than this can be implied in loving as Christ
loved his Church when he gave himself for it.

This love implies *the utmost gentleness in manner*. One
may be very faithful and true and yet lack that
affectionateness in speech and act which has such power to
satisfy the heart. One of the special Scripture admonitions
to husbands is that they love their wives and be not bitter
against them. It is a counsel against all display of ill-temper,
all bitter feelings as well as angry words and unkind acts.
The teaching of the passage strictly interpreted is that all
bitterness should be suppressed in the very workings of the
heart and changed into sweetness.

Are all husbands blameless in this respect? Are there
none who are sometimes bitter against their wives? Are
there none who sometimes speak sharp words that strike

and sting like arrows in their hearts? It must be in thoughtlessness, for no true man who really loves his wife would intentionally cause her pain. The poet Cowper suggested a very subtle test of character when he wrote—

"I would not enter on my list of friends,
Though graced with manners and fine sense
(Yet wanting sensibility), the man
Who needlessly sets foot upon a worm."

Yet there are men who would not willingly tread upon a crawling insect or a worm, who would not injure a dumb animal nor needlessly hurt any of the lowest of God's creatures, who every day bring many a pang to the heart of the tender, faithful, loving wife of their bosom by their sharp words or their impatient looks or acts.

The trouble is that men fall into free and careless habits at home. They are not so in society; they are gentle to other women. They pride themselves on their thoughtfulness. They are careful not even by tone or look to hurt a sensitive spirit. But at home too often they are rude, careless in speech and heedless of the effect of their words and actions. They blurt out in their own houses the ill-humor they have suppressed all day on the street. They answer proper questions in an irritated tone. They speak impatiently on the slightest provocation. They are sullen, morose and unsocial. They forget that their own wives are women with gentle spirits, easily hurt. A man thinks that because a woman is his wife she should understand him, that she should know that he loves her even if he is rude to her, that she should not mind anything he says or does, even if it is something that would sorely hurt or offend any other woman.

There never was a falser premise than this. Just because she is his wife he owes her the loftiest courtesy that is in his nature to pay. There is no other woman in all the world that feels so keenly the sting of sharp or thoughtless words from his lips as his own wife, and there is no other of whose feelings he should be so careful and whom he should so grieve to hurt. No other has the claim upon his thoughtfulness and affection that she has. Love gives no license for rudeness or incivility to the one who is loved. The closer the relationship, the more are hearts pained by any look, tone, gesture or word that tells of bitterness or even of thoughtlessness.

But it is not enough that men be not bitter against their wives. The mere absence of a fault or vice is not a virtue. Silence is no doubt better than bitterness. Even stateliness, though cold as a marble statue, is possibly better than rudeness. A garden without weeds, though having neither plant nor flower, is better than a patch of weeds; but a garden beautiful and fragrant with flowers is better still. It is a step in the right direction when a husband is not bitter against his wife, and it is a good deal farther in the right direction when instead of being bitter, his words and acts and whole bearing are characterized by gentleness and affectionateness. There are men who speak no bitter words, no sharp petulant words, and yet but few kindly, tender words fall from their lips. The old warmth of the lover and the newly-wed husband has died out and the speech is business-like and cold. No one needs to be told that there is nothing in such a bearing to satisfy a heart that craves the richest things true love can give.

Words seem little things, so fleeting and evanescent that apparently it cannot matter much of what sort they are. They are so easily spoken that we forget what power they have to give pleasure or pain. They seem so swiftly gone that we forget they do not go away at all, but linger either like barbed arrows in the heart where they struck, or like fragrant flowers distilling perfume. They seem so powerless for good or ill, and we do not remember that they either tear down or build up fair fabrics of joy and peace in the souls of those to whom we speak. They drop from our lips and are gone forever, as it appears to us;

"Yet, on the dull silence breaking
With a lightning flush, a word,
Bearing endless desolation
On its blighting wings, I heard;

Earth can forge no keener weapon,
Dealing surer death and pain;
And the cruel echo answered
Through long years again.
I have known one word hung starlike
O'er a dreary waste of years,
And it only shone the brighter
Looked at through a mist of tears,
While a weary wanderer gathered
Hope and heart on life's dark way
By its faithful promise shining
Clearer day by day."

While gentleness should always mark a husband's bearing toward his wife, there are occasions which call for peculiar thoughtfulness and sympathetic expression. Sometimes she is very weary. The cares of the day have been unusually trying. Matters have not gone smoothly at home. Her quivering nerves have been sorely overtaxed. She has heard sad news. A child has been sick all day, or, worse still, has by some disobedience or some wrong-doing almost broken her heart. What is a husband's part at such times? Surely if he is capable of tenderness he will allow it now. He will not utter a word to add to the load the overburdened spirit is already carrying. He will seek rather by every thoughtful help his love can give to lighten the burden, to quiet the trembling heart and to impart strength and peace.

In walking on the street one day in a violent and sudden storm, as I was passing under a tree, a weary bird fluttered down from among the branches, and alighting on my bosom crept under my coat. It was seeking a refuge from the fierce storm. Every wife should know that she will always find in her husband's love a safe and quiet refuge when she is perplexed or tried. She should be sure that he will understand her, that he will deal most gently with her, that he will give his own strength to shelter her, that he will impart of his own life to build up the waste in hers. She should never have to doubt that he will sympathize with her in whatever it may be that tries her. She should never have to fear repulse or coldness or rebuke when she flees to him for shelter. What Christ is to his people in their weariness, their sorrow, their pain, their alarm, every husband in his own little measure should be to his own wife.

There is one place where we shall remember every unkindness and every neglect shown to those who lean upon us for support and for sympathy, and then the pain will be ours if we have failed in tenderness. Ruskin says: "He who has once stood beside the grave, to look back upon the companions on whom it has been forever closed, feeling how impotent *there* is the wild love or the keen sorrow to give one instant's pleasure to the pulseless heart, or atone in the lowest measure to the departed spirit for the hour of unkindness, will scarcely for the future incur that debt to the heart which can only be discharged to the dust." Yet how slow we all are to learn this lesson!

It is of little avail to bring flowers to a wife's coffin when you failed to strew flowers on the path while her weary feet were painfully walking over it. It is of little avail to speak her praises now in every ear, to recount her excellences and dwell upon her virtues, when in her lifetime you never found a word of praise for her own ears, nor a loving compliment nor any token to show to her how much you prized her.

> "You placed this flower in her hand, you say,
> This pure, pale rose in her hand of clay?
> Methinks, could she lift her sealed eyes
> They would meet your own with a grieved surprise.
> "When did you give her a flower before?
> Ah, well, what matter when all is o'er?
>
>   *   *   *   *
>
> "But I pray you, think, when some fairer face
> Shines like a star from a wonted place,
> That love will starve if it is not fed—
> That true hearts pray for their daily bread."

The time to show love's tenderness is when it is needed; if we have failed then, the duty never can be rendered at all. No after-atonement of lavish affection can brighten the hours that were left unbrightened in passing, or lighten the burdens that were left unlightened when the weary spirit was bowing under them.

The spirit of this love requires a husband to *honor* his wife. He honored her before she was his wife. He saw in her his ideal of all that was noble, lovely and queenly. He showed her every mark of honor of which his soul was capable. Now that he has lifted her up to the throne of his heart will he honor her less? Not less, but more and ever more, if he be a true husband and a manly man. He has taken her now into the closest and holiest relation of earth. He has linked her life with his own, so that henceforward whatever affects one affects both. If one is honored the other is exalted; if one is dishonored the other is debased. There is infinitely more reason why he should honor her now than before she was his wife.

The ways in which he should show her honor are countless. He will do it by providing for her wants on as generous a scale as his position and his means will justify. He will do it by making her the sharer of all his own life. He will counsel with her about his business, advise with her concerning every new plan, and confide to her at every point the results of his undertakings. A true wife is not a child. When he chose her to be his wife he believed her to be worthy. She may not have all of his wisdom with regard to the affairs of business, but she may be able to make many a suggestion which will prove valuable, for women's quick intuition often sees at a glance what men's slow logic is long in discovering. Many a man owes to his wife's wise counsel a large measure of his success. And there is many another man whose success would have been greater, or to whom failure would not have come, if he had sought or accepted his wife's help.

But even if she is not qualified to give him great aid in his business plans, she loves him and is deeply interested in everything that he is doing. She is made happy by being taken into all his counsels, and thus lifted up close beside him in his life-work; and he is made stronger, too, for energetic duty and for heroic achievement by her warm sympathy and by the inspiration of her cheerful encouragement. Whether the day bring defeat or victory, failure or success, he should confide all to her in the evening. If the day has been prosperous she has a right to share the gratification; if it has been adverse, she will want, as a true wife, to help her husband bear his burden and to whisper a new word of courage in his heart. Not only then does a man fail to give his wife due honor when he shuts her out of his own business life; but he also robs himself of that inspiration and help which every true wife is able to minister to her husband.

It need scarcely even be said, further, that a husband should honor his wife by being worthy of her. Love has been the inspiration that has lifted many a man from a lowly place to lofty heights of worth or power. Many a youth of humble origin and without rank or condition has worshiped at the feet of a maiden far above him in social standing, and, incited by his ardent affection, has made himself worthy of her and then won her as his bride.

Quintin Matsys, the celebrated painter, was in his youth a blacksmith at Antwerp. He loved the beautiful daughter of a painter and was loved in return; but her father was inexorable. "Wert thou a painter," he said, "she should be thine; but a blacksmith—never!" The young man was not discouraged. The hammer dropped from his hand. A new life began to stir within him. A thousand glorious conceptions began to flit like shadows across his brain. "I will be a painter," he said. He thought of his utter ignorance of art, without any technical knowledge, and was cast down at first. But he began, and his first efforts encouraged him. He took the pencil, and the lines that came were the features of the face that glowed in his heart. Inspired by love he wrought on. "I will paint her portrait," he said; and the colors flashed upon his canvas till the likeness was perfect. He took it to the father. "There," said he, "I claim the prize, for I am a painter now." He won his bride by making himself worthy of her. Under the inspiration of love he continued to paint, winning new victories of genius, becoming eminent among artists, and, dying, was buried with high honors in the cathedral of his native city. The grand motive of his life was to become worthy of her whom he desired to win.

Every true-hearted husband should seek to be worthy of the wife he has already won. For her sake he should reach out after the noblest achievements and strive to attain the loftiest heights of character. To her he is the ideal of all that is manly, and he should seek to become every day more worthy of the homage she pays to him. Every possibility in his soul should be developed. Every latent power and energy of his life should be brought out. His hand should be trained under love's inspiration to do its most skillful work. Every fault in his character should be eradicated, every evil habit conquered, and every hidden beauty of soul should burst into fragrant bloom for her sake. She looks to him as her ideal of manhood, and he must see to it that the ideal is never marred, that he never falls by any unworthy act of his own from the high pedestal in her heart to which she has raised him. Among all sins few are worse than those by which a man draws down shame and reproach upon himself, for, besides all the sorrow he brings upon her in so many other ways, he thus crushes in his wife's heart the fair and noble image of manhood which she had enshrined there next to her Saviour's.

In the spirit of this love every husband should be *a large-hearted man*. He should never be a tyrant, playing the petty despot in his home. There is no surer mark than this of a small man. A manly man has a generous spirit which shows itself in all his life, but nowhere so richly as within his own doors. There are wives whose natures do not blossom out in their best beauty because the atmosphere in which they live is chill and cold. A lady who is always watching for beautiful things and gathering them about her brought from the mountain a sod of moss. She put it in her parlor, and after a while, in the genial warmth there sprang out from the bosom of the moss a multitude of sweet, delicate spring flowers. The seeds had long lain in the moss but in the cold air of the mountain they had never burst into life. There are noble wives in homes humble and homes stately who are just like this moss. In their natures there are the germs of many excellences and the possibilities of rich outcome, but the home-atmosphere is repressing and chilly, and in it none of these richer qualities and powers manifest themselves. The bringing of new warmth into the home will draw out these latent germs of unsuspected loveliness. The husband who would have his wife's nature blossom out into its best possibilities of character, influence and power must make a genial summer atmosphere for his home all the round year.

Then this large-heartedness will impart its spirit to the

home itself. A husband who is generous within his own doors will not be close and niggardly outside. The heart that is used always to be open at home cannot be carried shut through this suffering world. The prosperous home of a gentleman sends many a blessing and comfort out to less-favored homes. Every true home ought to be a help to a great many struggling lives. Every generous and large-hearted man scatters many a comfort among the needy and the suffering as he passes through this world.

There is nothing lost by such scattering. No richer blessing can come upon a home than the benedictions of those who have been helped, who have been fed at its doors, or sheltered beneath its roof, or inspired by its cheer and kindly interest. There is no memorial that any man can make for himself in this world so lasting and so satisfying as that which a life of unselfish kindness and beneficence builds up.

There is an old legend of the white hand. There was a king who gloried not in pomp and power, but in deeds of love. He scattered blessings everywhere. He took the food from his own table and gave it to the poor. Nothing in his possession was withheld when human need cried in his ear. He would give the last he had to help some suffering one.

One day a bishop seized the royal hand and blessed it, saying, "May this fair hand, this bountiful hand, never grow old!" Soon after this war came and the king was slain in battle. His conqueror gave command to sever his limbs and expose them to view, according to the cruel custom of the time, on poles and stakes. It was done, but that hand which had thus been blessed, and which had wrought so many beautiful deeds of love, when all else had perished in the bleaching sun remained unblemished, unwasted, wondrous white and fair, pointing still upward toward heaven as if raised in prayer.

The legend teaches that the hands and hearts which give out blessings to others in the Master's name and for his sake, that minister comfort, joy, help, healing and uplifting, that make others happier, stronger, safer, better, shall remain for ever pure and white in the heaven of glory, when earthly honors have faded and crowns and jewels have mouldered.

One thing more may be said: Every husband of a Christian wife should walk with her in common love for Christ. There are some husbands, however, who fail in this. They love their wives very sincerely, and make many sacrifices for their sake. They carefully shelter them from life's rude blasts. They bless them with all tenderness and affectionateness. They honor them very highly, bringing many a noble achievement to lay at their feet, and showing them all homage and respect. They do everything that love can suggest to make their earthly happiness full and complete. They share every burden and walk close beside them in every way of trial. But when they come to the matter of personal religion they draw back and leave them to go alone. While the wife goes into the sanctuary to worship the husband waits without. At the very point where his interest in her life should be deepest it fails altogether.

Surely it is a great wrong to a woman, tender and dependent, to leave her to walk alone through this world in her deepest life, receiving no sympathy, no companionship, no support, from him who is her dearest friend. She must leave him outside of the most sacred part of her life. She must be silent to him concerning the experiences of her soul in its spiritual struggles, aspirations, yearnings, hopes. She must bear alone the responsibility of the children's religious nurture and training. Alone she must bow in prayer before God. Alone she must sit at the Lord's table.

It cannot be right that a husband should leave his wife to live such a large part of her life without his companionship and sympathy. His love should seek to enter with her into every sacred experience. In no other way could he give her such joy as by taking his place beside her as a fellow-heir of the same grace. It would lighten every burden, since he would now share it with her. It would bring new radiance to her face, new peace to her heart, new zest to all life for her. It would make their marriage more perfect and unite their hearts in a closer union, since only those realize the full sweetness of wedded life who are one at every point and in every feeling, purpose and hope, and whose souls blend in their higher, spiritual part as well as in their lower nature and experiences. Then it would also introduce the husband himself to sources of blessing and strength of which he has never known before; for the religion of Christ is a reality and brings the soul into communication with God and with infinite springs of comfort, help and blessing. In sharing her life of faith and prayer he would find his own life linked to heaven.

United, then, on earth in a common faith in Christ, their mutual love mingling and blending in the love of God, they shall be united also in heaven in eternal fellowship. Why should hearts spend years on earth in growing into one, knitting life to life, blending soul in soul, for a union that is not to reach beyond the valley of shadows? Why not weave for eternity?

THE WIFE'S PART

It is a high honor for a woman to be chosen from among all womankind to be the wife of a good and true man. She is lifted up to be a crowned queen. Her husband's manly love laid at her feet exalts her to the throne of his life. Great power is placed in her hands. Sacred dispositions are reposed in her keeping. Will she wear her crown beneficently? Will she fill her realm with beauty and with blessing? Or will she fail in her holy trust? Only her married life can be the answer.

A woman may well pause before she gives her hand in marriage, and inquire whether he is worthy to whom she is asked to surrender so much; whether he can bring true happiness to her life; whether he can meet the cravings of her nature for love and for companionship; whether he is worthy to be lifted to the highest place in her heart and honored as a husband should be honored. She must ask these questions for her own sake, else the dream may fade with the bridal wreath, and she may learn, when too late, that he for whom she has left all and to whom she has given all is not worthy of the sacred trust, and has no power to fill her life with happiness, to wake her heart's chords to touch her soul's depths.

But the question should be turned and asked from the other side. Can she be a true wife to win who asks for her hand? Is she worthy of the love that is laid at her feet? Can she be a blessing to the life of him who would lift her to the throne of his heart? Will he find in her all the beauty, all the tender loveliness, all the rich qualities of nature, all the deep sympathy and companionship, all the strengthful, uplifting love, all the sources of joy and help, which he seems now to see in her? Is there any possible future for him which she could not share? Are there needs in his soul, or hungers, which she cannot answer? Are there chords in his life which her fingers cannot wake?

Surely it is proper for her to question her own soul for him while she bids him question his soul for her. A wife has a part in the song of wedded love if it is to be a harmony. She holds in her hands on her wedding day precious interests, sacred destinies and holy responsibilities, which, if disclosed to her sight at once, might well appall the bravest heart. Her opportunity is one which the loftiest angel might covet. Not the happiness only of a manly life, but its whole future of character, of influence, of growth, rests with her.

Look at a pen-picture of a good wife by a master:

"A good wife is Heaven's last, best gift to man, his
angel and minister of graces innumerable, his gem of
many virtues; her voice his sweetest music, her smiles
his brightest day, her kiss the guardian of his innocence,
her arms the pale of his safety, the balm of his health,
the sure balsam of his life; her industry his surest
wealth, her economy his safest steward, her lips his
faithful counselor, her bosom the softest pillow of his
cares, and her prayers the ablest advocate of Heaven's
blessing on his head."

If that is what a wife is to be to her husband, is there no
need for a woman to question her soul before she goes to
the marriage altar?

What is the true ideal of a wife? It is not something
lifted above the common experiences of life, not an ethereal
angel feeding on ambrosia and moving in the realms of
fancy. In some European cities they sell to the tourist
models of their cathedrals made of alabaster, whiter than
snow. But so delicate are these alabaster shrines that they
must be kept under glass covers or they will be soiled by the
dust, and so frail that they must be sheltered from every
rude touch, lest their lovely columns may be shattered.
They are very graceful and beautiful, but they serve no lofty
purpose. No worshipers can enter their doors. No melody
rises to heaven from their aisles. So there are ideals of

womanhood which are very lovely, full of graceful charms, pleasing, attractive, but which are too delicate and frail for this prosaic, storm-swept world of ours. Such ideals the poets and the novelists sometimes give us. They appear well to the eye as they are portrayed for us on the brilliant page. But of what use would they be in the life which the real woman of our day has to live? A breath of earthly air would stain them. One day of actual experience in the hard toils and sore struggles of life would shatter their frail loveliness to fragments. We had better seek for ideals which will not be soiled by a rude touch nor blown away by a stiff breeze, and which will grow lovelier as they move through life's paths of sacrifice and toil. The true wife needs to be no mere poet's dream, no artist's picture, no ethereal lady too little for use, but a woman healthful, strong, practical, industrious, with a hand for life's common duties, yet crowned with that beauty which a high and noble purpose gives to a soul.

One of the first essential elements in a wife is *faithfulness*—faithfulness, too, in the largest sense. "The heart of her husband doth safely trust in her." Perfect confidence is the basis of all true affection. A shadow of doubt destroys the peace of married life. A true wife by her character and by her conduct proves herself worthy of her husband's trust. He has confidence in her affection; he knows that her heart is unalterably true to him. He has confidence in her management; he confides to her the care of his household. He knows that she is true to all his interests—that she is prudent and wise, not wasteful nor extravagant. It is one of the essential things in a true wife that her husband shall be able to leave in her hands the management of all domestic affairs, and know that they are safe. Wifely thriftlessness and extravagance have destroyed the happiness of many a household and wrecked many a home. On the other hand, many a man owes his prosperity to his wife's prudence and her wise administration of household affairs.

Every true wife makes her husband's interests her own. While he lives for her, carrying her image in his heart and toiling for her all the days, she thinks only of what will do him good. When burdens press upon him she tries to lighten them by sympathy, by cheer, by the inspiration of love. She enters with zest and enthusiasm into all his plans. She is never a weight to drag him down; she is strength in his heart to help him ever to do nobler and better things.

All wives are not such blessings to their husbands. Woman is compared sometimes to the vine, while man is the strong oak to which it clings. But there are different kinds of vines. Some wreathe a robe of beauty and a crown of glory for the tree, covering it in summer days with green leaves and in the autumn hanging among its branches rich purple clusters of fruit; others twine their arms about it only to sap its very life and destroy its vigor, till it stands decaying and unsightly, stripped of its splendor, discrowned and fit only for the fire.

A true wife makes a man's life nobler, stronger, grander, by the omnipotence of her love "turning all the forces of manhood upward and heavenward." While she clings to him in holy confidence and loving dependence she brings out in him whatever is noblest and richest in his being. She inspires him with courage and earnestness. She beautifies his life. She softens whatever is rude and harsh in his habits or his spirit. She clothes him with the gentler graces of refined and cultured manhood. While she yields to him and never disregards his lightest wish, she is really his queen, ruling his whole life and leading him onward and upward in every proper path.

But there are wives also like the vines which cling only to blight. Their dependence is weak, indolent helplessness. They lean but impart no strength. They cling but they sap the life. They put forth no hand to help. They loll on sofas or promenade the streets; they dream over sentimental novels; they gossip in drawing-rooms. They are utterly useless, and being useless they become burdens even to manliest, tenderest love. Instead of making a man's life stronger, happier, richer, they absorb his strength, impair his usefulness, hinder his success and cause him to be a failure among men. To themselves also the result is wretchedness. Dependence is beautiful when it does not become weakness and inefficiency. The true wife clings and leans; but she also helps and inspires. Her husband feels the mighty inspiration of her love in all his life. Toil is easier, burdens are lighter, battles are less fierce, because of the face that waits in the quiet of the home, because of the heart that beats in loving sympathy whatever the experience, because of the voice that speaks its words of cheer and encouragement when the day's work is done. No wife knows how much she can do to make her husband honored among men, and his life a power and a success, by her loyal faithfulness, by the active inspiration of her own sweet life. Here are true words from another pen:

"The woodman's axe swings lighter, the heavy blows on the anvil have more music than fatigue in them, the farmer whistles cheerfully over his plough, the mechanic's severest toil is lightened by a sweet refrain, when he knows that his fair young bride is in sympathy with him, and while watching his return is providing daintily for his pleasure and comfort, eager to give him loving welcome. To the artist at his easel come fairer visions to be transformed to the canvas because of the dear one presiding over his house. The author in his study finds the dullest subjects clothed in freshness and vigor because of the gentle critic to whom he can go for aid and encouragement. The lawyer prepares his case with better-balanced energy, thinks more clearly, pleads his cause with more effective eloquence, inspired by the cheering words uttered as he goes to his labors by the young wife whose thoughts he is assured will follow his work with her judicious, tranquilizing sympathy. The physician in his daily rounds among the sick and suffering knows there is one, now all his own, praying for his success, and this knowledge so fills his being that his very presence by the sick bed has healing in it. The young pastor in his efforts to minister to the spiritual wants of his flock will speak peace to the troubled souls committed to his trust with far more zeal and tenderness for the love that will smile on him when he returns home."

The good wife is *a good housekeeper*. I know well how unromantic this remark will appear to those whose dreams of married life are woven of the fancies of youthful sentiment, but these frail dreams of sentiment will not last long amid the stern realities of life, and then that which will prove one of the rarest elements of happiness and blessing in the household will be housewifely industry and diligence.

A Greek philosopher, walking at night and gazing up at the sky, stumbled and fell. His companion observed: "One should not have his head in the stars while his feet are on the earth." There are some wives who commit the same mistake. They set their eyes on romantic ideals and neglect the real duties that come close to their hands, in which the true secret of happiness and blessing lies. They have their eyes and head among the stars while their feet are walking on mundane soil, and no wonder if they stumble. It may be put down as a positive rule, whether among the rich or the poor, whether in a palace or in a cottage, that the wife who would be happy, and make her home happy and permanently beautiful, must work with her hands at the housewifely tasks which the days in turn bring to her.

When young people marry they are rarely troubled with many thoughts about the details of housekeeping. Their dreams are high above all such commonplaces. The mere mention of such things as cooking, baking, sweeping, dusting, mending, ironing, jars upon the poetic rhythm of the lofty themes of conversation. It never enters the brains of these happy lovers that it can make any difference in the world in their home-life whether the bread is sweet or sour, whether the oatmeal is well cooked or scorched, whether the meals are punctual or tardy. The mere thought that such sublunary matters could affect the tone of their wedded life seems a desecration.

It is a pity to dash away such exquisite dreams, but the truth is they do not long outlast the echo of the wedding peals or the fragrance of the bridal roses. The newly married are not long within their own doors before they find that something more than tender sentiment is needed to make their home-life a success. They come down from the clouds when the daily routine begins and touch the common soil on which the feet of other mortals walk. Then they find that they are dependent, just like ordinary people, on some quite prosaic conditions. One of the very first things they discover is the intimate relation between the kitchen and wedded happiness. That love may fulfill its delightful prophecies and realize its splendid dreams there must be in the new home a basis of material and very practical elements. The palace that is to rise into the air, shooting up its towers, displaying its wonders of architecture, flashing its splendors in the sunshine, the admiration of the world, must have its foundation in commonplace earth, resting on plain, hard, honest rock. Love may build its palace of noble sentiments and tender affections and sweet charities, rising into the very clouds, and in this splendid home two souls may dwell in the enjoyment of the highest possibilities of wedded life; but this palace, too, must stand on the ground, with unpoetic and unsentimental stones for its foundation. That foundation is *good housekeeping*. In other words, good breakfasts, dinners and suppers, a well-kept house, order, system, promptness, punctuality, good cheer—far more than any young lovers—dream does happiness in married life depend upon such commonplace things as these. Love is very patient, very kind, very gentle; and where there is love no doubt the plainest fare is ambrosia and the homeliest surroundings are charming. I know the wise man said: "Better is a dinner of herbs where love is, than a stalled ox (i.e., a good roast-beef dinner), with hatred therewith;" but herbs as a constant diet will pall on the taste, especially if poorly served, even if love is ever present to season them. In this day of advanced civilization it ought to be possible to have both the stalled ox and love. Husbands are not angels in this mundane state, and not being such they need a substantial basis of good housekeeping for the realization of their dreams of blissful homemaking.

Here is a paragraph worth quoting: "The spirit of wedded love may regard the house, in its completeness of appointment and wisdom of management, as only the outer shell, worthless except when vitalized by the heart into a living home; but it must not forget that its delicate life needs sheathing in this outer order of the house—the temple-walls around the inner altar—that its heaven-lighted fire may be guarded from being chilled down by dampening worries or blown out by gusty tempers. The house with its provision for the daily needs of the lower life, duly ordered and graciously illumined, is the trellis within which affections intertwine, and loving hearts, growing out into efflorescent richness, build up the home. Where a strengthful womanhood keeps the house wisely and well, in prudent care and orderly comfort and cheerful peace, there, in the daily duties, trying and tasting, her character issues in loveliness of bloom and blessedness of privilege, softly shadowing the household beneath its gracious power and unselfish gentleness; so that the heart of her husband rejoiceth in her, and the love which was planted within those walls strikes down its roots through all thin-soiled fancy and passion into the rich ground of manly reverence and honor, from which to draw a sustenance and life which shall keep it fresh and green in the midst of the years as those that are planted in the house of the Lord."

There certainly have been cases in which very tender love has lost its tenderness and when the cause lay in the disorder, the negligence and the mismanagement of the housewifery. There is no doubt that many a heart-estrangement begins at the table where meals are unpunctual and food is poorly cooked or repulsively served. Bad housekeeping will soon drive the last vestige of romance out of any home. The illusion which love weaves about an idolized bride will soon vanish if she proves incompetent in her domestic management. The wife who will keep the charm of early love unbroken through the years, and in whose home the dreams of the wedding-day will come true, must be a good housekeeper.

In one of his Epistles St. Paul gives the counsel that young wives should be "workers at hcme," as the Revisers have put it, signifying that home is the sphere of the wife's duties, and that she is to find her chief work there. There is a glory in all the Christian charities which Christian women, especially in these recent days, are founding and conducting with so much enthusiasm and such marked and abounding success. Woman is endowed with gifts of sympathy, of gentleness, of inspiring strengthfulness, which peculiarly fit her to be Christ's messenger of mercy to human woe and sorrow and pain.

"The mission of woman on earth! To give birth
To the mercy of heaven descending on earth.
The mission of woman permitted to bruise
The head of the serpent, and sweetly infuse
Through the sorrow and sin of earth's registered curse
The blessing which mitigates all: born to nurse,
And to soothe, and to solace, to help and to heal
The sick world that leans on her."

There is the widest opportunity in the most fitting service for every woman whose heart God has touched to be a ministering angel to those who need sympathy or help. There are many who are free to serve in public charities, in caring for the poor, for the sick in hospital wards, for the orphaned and the aged. There are few women who cannot do a little in some one or more of these organizations of Christian beneficence.

But it should be understood that for every wife the first duty is the making and keeping of her own home. Her first and best work should be done there, and till it is well done she has no right to go outside to take up other duties. She is to be a "worker at home." She must look upon her home as the one spot on earth for which she alone is responsible, and which she must cultivate well for God if she never does anything outside. For her the Father's business is not attending Dorcas societies and missionary meetings, and mothers' meetings, and temperance conventions, or even teaching a Sunday-school class, until she has made her own home all that her wisest thought and best skill can make it. There have been wives who in their zeal for Christ's work outside have neglected Christ's work inside their own doors. They have had eyes and hearts for human need and human sorrow in the broad fields lying far out, but neither eye nor heart for the work of love lain about their own feet. The result has been that while they were doing angelic work in the lanes and streets, the angels were mourning over their neglected duties within the hallowed walls of their own homes. While they were winning a place in the hearts of the poor or the sick or the orphan, they were losing their rightful place in the hearts of their own household. Let it be remembered that Christ's work in the home is the first that he gives to every wife, and that no amount of consecrated activities in other spheres will atone in this world or the next for neglect or failure there.

The good wife is *generous and warm-hearted*. She does

not grow grasping and selfish. In her desire to economize and add to her stores she does not forget those who suffer or want. While she gives her wisest and most earnest thought and her best and most skillful work to her own home, her heart does not grow cold toward those outside who need sympathy. I cannot conceive of true womanhood ripened into mellow richness, yet wanting the qualities of gentleness and unselfishness. A woman whose heart is not touched by the sickness of sorrow and whose hands do not go out in relief where it is in her power to help, lacks one of the elements which make the glory of womanhood.

This is not the place to speak of woman as a ministering angel. If it were it would be easy to fill many pages with the bright records of most holy deeds of self-sacrifice. I am speaking now, however, of woman as wife; and only upon too much of this ministry to the suffering as she may perform in her own home, at her own door and in connection with her housewifely duties is it fit to finger at this time. But even in this limited sphere her opportunities are by no means small.

It is in her own home that this warmth of heart and this openness of hand are first to be shown. It is as wife and mother that her gentleness performs its most sacred ministry. Her hand wipes away the tear-drops when there is sorrow. In sickness, she is the tender nurse. She bears upon her own heart every burden that weighs upon her husband.

No matter how the world goes with him during the day, when he enters his own door he meets the fragrant atmosphere of love. Other friends may forsake him, but she clings to him with unalterable fidelity. When gloom comes down and adversity falls upon him, her faithful eyes look ever into his like two stars of hope shining in the darkness. When his heart is crushed, beneath her smile it gathers itself again into strength, "like a wind-torn flower in the sunshine." "You cannot imagine," wrote De Tocqueville of his wife, "what she is in great trials. Usually so gentle, she then becomes strong and energetic. She watches me without my knowing it; she softens, calms and strengthens me in difficulties which distract me, but leave her serene." An eloquent tribute, but one which thousands of husbands might give. Men often see not the angel in the plain, plodding woman who walks quietly beside them, until the day of trial comes: then in the darkness the glory shines out. An angel ministered to our Lord when in Gethsemane he wrestled with his great and bitter sorrow. What a benediction to the mighty sufferer was in the soft gliding to his side of that gentle presence, in the touch of that soothing, supporting hand laid upon him, in the comfort of that gentle voice thrilling with sympathy as it spoke its strengthening message of love! Was it a mere coincidence that just at that time and in that place the radiant messenger came? No, it is always so. Angels choose such occasions to pay their visits to men.

"With silence only as their benediction
God's angels come,
Where in the shadow of a great affliction
The soul sits dumb."

So it is in the dark hours of a man's life, when burdens press, when sorrows weigh like mountains upon his soul, when adversities have left him crushed and broken, or when he is in the midst of fierce struggles which try the strength of every fibre of his manhood, that all the radiance and glory of a true wife's strengthful love shine out before his eyes. Only then does he recognize in her God's angel of mercy.

O woman! in our hours of ease
Uncertain, coy, and hard to please,
And variable as the shade
By the light quivering aspen made;
When pain and anguish wring the brow,
A ministering angel thou!"

In sickness how thoughtful, how skillful, how gentle a nurse is the true wife! In struggles with temptation or adversity or difficulty, what an inspiration she is! In misfortune or disaster, what lofty heroism does she exhibit and what courage does her bravery kindle in her husband's heart! Instead of being crushed by the unexpected loss, she only then rises to her full grandeur of soul. Instead of weeping, repining and despairing, and thus adding tenfold to the burden of the misfortune, she cheerfully accepts the changed circumstances and becomes a minister of hope and strength. She turns away from luxury and ease to the plainer home, the simpler life, the humbler surroundings—without a murmur. It is in such circumstances and experiences that the heroism of woman's soul is manifested. Many a man is carried victoriously through misfortune and enabled to rise again, because of the strong inspiring sympathy and the self-forgetting help of his wife; and many a man fails in fierce struggle, and rises not again from the defeat of misfortune, because the wife at his side proves unequal to her opportunity.

But a wife's ministry of mercy reaches outside her own doors. Every true home is an influence of blessing in the community where it stands. Its lights shine out. Its songs ring out. Its spirit breathes out. The neighbors know whether it is hospitable or inhospitable, warm or cold, inviting or repelling. Some homes bless no lives outside their own circle; others are perpetually pouring out sweetness and fragrance. The ideal Christian home is a far-reaching benediction. It sets its lamps in the windows, and while they give no less light and cheer to those within, they pour a little beam upon the gloom without, which may brighten some dark path and put a little cheer into the heart of some belated passer-by. Its doors stand ever open with a welcome to every one who comes seeking shelter from the storm, or sympathy in sorrow, or help in trial. It is a hospice, like those blessed refuges on the Alps, where the weary or the chilled or the fainting are sure always of refreshment, of warmth, of kindly friendship, of gentle ministry, of mercy. It is a place where one who is in trouble may go confident ever of sympathy and comfort. It is a place where the young people love to go, because they know they are welcome and because they find inspiration and help there.

And this spirit of the home the wife makes; indeed, it is her own spirit filling the house and pouring out like light or like fragrance. A true wife is universally beloved. She is recognized as one of God's angels scattering blessings as far as her hand can reach. Her neighbors are all blessed by her ministrations. When sickness or sorrow touches any other household, some token of sympathy finds its way from her hand into the shadowed home. To the old she is gentle and patient. To the young she is inciting and helpful. To the poor she is God's hand reached out. To the sufferer she brings strength. To the sorrowing she is a consoler. There is trouble nowhere near but her face appears at the door and her hand brings its benediction.

I quote a few words from Mr. Arnot: "They call woman

sometimes, in thoughtless flattery, an angel, but here an angel in sober truth she is, a messenger sent by God to assuage the sorrows of humanity. The worn traveler who has come through the desert with his life and nothing more; the warrior faint and bleeding from the battle; the distressed of every age and country—long instinctively for this Heaven-provided help. Deep in the sufferer's nature, in the hour of his need, springs the desire to feel a woman's hand binding his wound or wiping his brow—to hear soft words dropping from a woman's lips. . . . Woman was needed in Eden; how much more in this thorny world outside! Physically, the vessel is weak, but in that very weakness her great strength lies. If knowledge is power in department, gentleness is power in woman's."

These are words that every wife should ponder. Every home should be a Bethesda, "a house of mercy," where the suffering, the weary, the sorrowful, the tempted, the tried, the fallen, may ever turn sure of sympathy, of help and of love's holiest fruits.

Two little stories of Elizabeth of Hungary illustrate this point and show the reward which such service brings. Her kindness to the sick and the poor was unbounded. Once she brought a leprous child to her palace and laid it in her own bed, because there was no other place to lay it. Her husband heard of it and came in some displeasure and drew down the cover of the bed to see if the object concealed there was really so loathsome as he had heard. And lo! instead of the festering and leprous body he saw the Saviour, radiant with glory, and turned away awe-stricken and yet glad. That was what Jesus said: "Inasmuch as ye have done it unto one of the least of these, ye have done it unto me." The ministries rendered to the poor, the suffering, the tempted, the sorrowing, are wrought as to Christ himself.

Some wife, weary already, her hands over-full with the multiplied cares and duties of her household life, may plead that she has no strength to spend in sympathy and help for others. But it is truly wonderful how light these added burdens seem when they are taken up in love. Another of these legends of Elizabeth tells that once she was bearing her cloak full of loaves to the poor whom she daily fed. Her husband met her, and being amazed at the size of the load she bore, looked to see what it was, and found only flowers. The loaves were as light as they were fragrant to the noble woman who carried them for the love she bore her Lord. So always the duties we perform out of love for him and his suffering ones become easy and pleasant as we take them up. Heaven's benediction rests ever on the home of her who lives to do good.

Scarcely a word has been said thus far of a wife's personal relation to her husband and the duties that spring out of that relation. These are manifested and yet they are so sacred and delicate that it seems hardly fit to speak or write of them. A few of the more important of these duties belonging to the wife's part may be merely touched upon.

A true wife gives her husband her fullest confidence. She hides nothing from him. She gives no pledge of secrecy which will seal her lips in his presence. She listens to no words of admiration from others which she may not repeat to him. She expresses to him every feeling, every hope, every desire and yearning, every joy or pain. Then while she utters every confidence in his ear she is most careful to speak in no other ear any word concerning the sacred inner life of her home. Are there little frictions or grievances in the wedded life? Has her husband faults which annoy her or cause her pain? Does he fail in this duty or that? Do differences arise which threaten the peace of the home? In the feeling of disappointment and pain, smarting under a sense of injury, a wife may be strongly tempted to seek sympathy by telling her trials to some intimate friends. Nothing could be more fatal to her own truest interests and to the hope of restored happiness and peace in her home. Grievances complained of outside remain unhealed sores. The wise wife will share her secret of unhappiness with none but her Master, while she strives in every way that patient love can suggest to remove the causes of discord or trouble.

Love sees much in a wife that other eyes see not. It throws a veil over her blemishes; it transfigures even her plainest features. One of the problems of her wedded life is to retain this charm for her husband's eyes as long as she lives, to appear lovely to him even when the color has faded from her cheeks and when the music has gone out of her voice. This is no impossibility; it is only what is done in every true home. But it cannot be done by the arts of the dressmaker, the milliner and the hair-dresser. Only the arts of love can do it. The wife who would always hold in her husband's heart the place she held on her wedding day will never cease striving to be lovely. She will be as careful of her words and acts and her whole bearing toward him as she was before marriage. She will cultivate in her own life whatever is beautiful, whatever is winning, whatever is graceful. She will scrupulously avoid whatever is offensive or unwomanly. She will look well to her personal appearance; no woman can be careless in her dress, slatternly and untidy, and long keep her place on the throne of her husband's life. She will look well to her inner life. She must have mental attractiveness. She will seek to be clothed in spiritual beauty. Her husband must see in her ever-new loveliness as the years move on. As the charms of physical beauty may fade in the toils and vicissitudes of life, there must be more and more beauty of soul to shine out to replace the attractions that are lost. It has been said that "the wife should always leave something to be revealed only to her husband, some modest charm, some secret grace, reserved solely for his delight and inspiration, like those flowers which give of their sweetness only to the hand that lovingly gathers them." She should always care more to please him than any other person in the world. She should prize more highly a compliment from his lips than from any other human lips. Therefore she should reserve for him the sweetest charms; she should seek to bring ever to him some new surprise of loveliness; she should plan pleasures and delights for him. Instead of not caring how she looks or whether she is agreeable or not when no one but her husband is present, she should always be at her best for him. Instead of being bright and lovely when there is company, then relapsing into languor and silence when the company is gone, she should seek always to be brightest and loveliest when only he and she sit together in the quiet of the home. Both husband and wife should ever bring their best things to each other.

Again let me say that no wife can overestimate the influence she wields over her husband, or the measure in which his character, his career and his very destiny are laid in her hands for shaping. The sway which she holds over him is the sway of love, but it is mighty and resistless. If she retains her power, if she holds her place as queen of his life, she can do with him as she will. Even unconsciously to herself, without any thought of her responsibility, she will exert over him an influence that will go far toward making or marring all his future. If she has no lofty conception of life herself, if she is vain and frivolous, she will only chill his ardor, weaken his resolution and draw him aside from any earnest endeavor. But if she has in her soul noble womanly qualities, if she has true thoughts of life, if she has purpose, strength of character and fidelity to principle, she will be to him an unfailing inspiration toward all that is noble, manly and Christlike. The high conceptions of life in her mind will elevate his conceptions. Her firm, strong purpose will put vigor and determination into every resolve and act of his. Her purity of soul will cleanse and refine his spirit. Her warm interest in all his affairs and her wise counsel at every point will make him strong for every duty and valiant in every struggle. Her careful domestic management will become an important element of success in his business life. Her bright, orderly, happy homemaking will be a perpetual source of joy and peace, and an incentive to nobler living. Her unwavering fidelity, her tender affectionateness, her womanly sympathy, her beauty of soul, will make her to him God's angel indeed, sheltering, guarding, keeping, guiding and blessing him. Just in the measure in which she realizes this lofty ideal of wifehood will she fulfill her mission and reap the rich harvest of her hopes.

Such is the "woman's lot" that falls on every wife. It is solemn enough to make her very thoughtful and very earnest. How can she make sure that her influence over her husband will be for good, that he will be a better man, more successful in his career and more happy, because she is his wife? Not by any mere moral posturing so as to seem to have lofty purpose and wise thoughts of life; not by any weak resolving to help him and be an uplifting inspiration to him; not by perpetual preaching and lecturing on a husband's duties and on manly character; she can do it only by being in the very depths of her soul, in every thought and impulse of her heart and in every fibre of her nature, a true and noble woman. She will make him not like what she tells him he ought to be, but like what she herself is.

So it all comes back to a question of character. She can be a good wife only by being a good woman and she can be a good woman in the true sense only by being a Christian woman. Nowhere save in Christ can she find the wisdom and strength she needs to meet the solemn responsibilities of wifehood. Only in Christ can she find that rich beauty of soul, that gemming and empearling of the character, which shall make her lovely in her husband's sight when the bloom of youth is gone, when the brilliance has faded out of her eyes and the roses have fled from her checks. Only Christ can teach her how to live so as to be blessed and a blessing in her married life.

Nothing in this world is sadder than to compare love's early dreams, what love meant to be, with the too frequent story of the after-life, what came of the dreams, what was the outcome of love's venture. Why so many sad disappointments? Why do so many bridal wreaths fall into dust? Is there no possibility of making these fair dreams come true, of keeping these flowers lovely and fragrant through all the years?

Yes, but only in Christ.

The young maiden goes smiling and singing to the marriage altar. Does she know that if she has not Christ with her she is as a lamb going to the sacrifice? Let her tarry at the gateway till she has linked her life to Him who is the first and the last. Human love is very precious, but it is not enough to satisfy a heart. There will be trials, there will be perplexities, there will be crosses and disappointments, there will be solicitudes and sorrows. Then none but Christ will be sufficient. Without him the way will be dreary. But with his benediction and presence the flowers that droop to-day will bloom fresh again to-morrow, and the dreams of early love will build themselves up into a Palace of peace and joy for the solace, the comfort and the shelter of old age.

THE PARENTS' PART

God has so constituted us that in loving and caring for our own children the richest and best things in our natures are drawn out. Many of the deepest and most valuable lessons ever learned are read from the pages of unfolding child-life. We best understand the feelings and affections of God toward us when we bend over our own child and see in our human parenthood a faint image of the divine Fatherhood. Then in the culture of character there is no influence more potent than that which touches us when our children are laid in our arms. Their helplessness appeals to every principle of nobleness in our hearts. Their innocence exerts over us a purifying power. The thought of our responsibility for them exalts every faculty of our souls. In the very care which they exact, they bring blessing to us. When old age comes, very lonely is the home which has neither son nor daughter to return with grateful ministries, to bring solace and comfort to the declining years!

It is a new marriage when the first-born enters the home. It draws the wedded lives together in a closeness they

have never known before. It touches chords in their hearts
that have lain silent until now. It calls out powers that have
never been exercised before. Hitherto unsuspected beauties
of character appear. The laughing heedless girl of a year ago
is transformed into a thoughtful woman. The careless,
unsettled youth leaps into manly strength and into
fixedness of character when he looks into the face of his
own child and takes it in his bosom. New aims rise up
before the young parents, new impulses begin to stir in
their hearts. Life takes on at once a new and deeper
meaning. The glimpse they have had into its solemn
mystery sobers them. The laying in their hands of a new
and sacred burden, an immortal life, to be guided and
trained by them, brings to them a sense of responsibility
that makes them thoughtful. Self is no longer the centre.
There is a new object to live for, an object great enough to
fill all their life and engross their highest powers. It is only
when the children come that life becomes real, that parents
begin to learn to live. We talk about training our children,
but they train us first, teaching us many a sacred lesson,
stirring up in us many a slumbering gift and possibility,
calling out many a hidden grace and disciplining our
wayward powers into strong and harmonious character.

"Children are God's apostles, day by day
Sent forth to preach of love, of hope, of peace."

Our homes would be very cold and dreary without the children. Sometimes we weary of their noise. They certainly bring us a great deal of care and solicitude. They cost us no end of toil. When they are very young they break our rest many a weary night with their colics and teethings, and when they grow older they well-nigh break our hearts many a time with their waywardness. After they come to us we may as well bid farewell to living for self and to personal ease and independence if we mean to do faithful duty as parents. There are some who therefore look upon the coming of children as a misfortune. They talk about them lightly as "responsibilities." They regard them as in the way of their pleasure. They see no blessing in them. But it is cold selfishness that looks upon children in this way. Instead of being hindrances to true and noble living, they are helps. They bring benedictions from heaven when they come, and while they stay they are perpetual benedictions.

> "Ah! what would the world be to us
> If the children were no more?
> We should dread the desert behind us
> Worse than the dark before.
>
> "What the leaves are to the forest,
> With light and air for food,

Ere their sweet and tender juices
Have been hardened into wood,—

"That to the world are children;
Through them it feels the glow
Of a brighter and sunnier climate
Than reaches the trunks below."

When the children come what shall we do with them? What duties do we owe to them? How may we discharge our responsibility? What is the parents' part in making the home and the home-life? It is impossible to overstate the importance of these questions.

"It is no little thing when a fresh soul
And a fresh heart, with their unmeasured scope
For good, not gravitating earthward yet,
But circling into diviner periods,
Are sent into this world."

It is a great thing to take these young and tender lives, rich with so many possibilities of beauty, of joy, of power, all of which may be wrecked, and to become responsible for their shaping and training and for the upbuilding of their character. This is what must be thought of in the making of a home. It must be a home in which children will grow up for true and noble life, for God and for heaven. Upon the parents the chief response rests. They are the builders of the home. From them it receives its character, whether good or evil. It will be just what they make it. If it be happy, they must be the authors of the happiness; if it be unhappy, the blame must rest with them. Its tone, its atmosphere, its spirit, its influence, it will take from them. They have the making of the home in their own hands, and God holds them responsible for it.

This responsibility rests upon both the parents. There are some fathers who seem to forget that any share of the burden and duty of making the home belongs to them. They leave it all to the mothers. They come and go as if they were scarcely more than boarders in their own house, with no active interest in the welfare of their children. They plead the demands of business as the excuse for their neglect. But where is the business that is so important as to justify a man's evasion of the sacred duties which he owes to his own family? There cannot be any other work in this world which a man can do that will excuse him at God's bar for having neglected the care of his own home and the training of his own children. No success in any department of the world's work can positively atone for failure here. No piling up of this world's treasures can compensate a man for the loss of those incomparable jewels, his own children.

In the prophet's parable he said to the king, "As thy

servant was busy here and there he was gone." May not this
be the only plea that some fathers will have to offer when
they stand before God without their children: "As I was
busy here and there they were gone." Men are busy in their
worldly affairs, busy pressing their plans and ambitions to
fulfillment, busy gathering money to lay up a fortune, busy
chasing the world's honors and building up a name, busy in
the quest for knowledge; and while they are busy, their
children grow up, and when they turn to see if they are
getting on well they are gone. Then they try most
earnestly to get them back again, but their intensest efforts
avail not. It is too late then to do that blessed work for
them and upon their lives which could so easily have been
done in their tender years. Dr. Geikie's book, entitled *Life*,
opens with these words: "Some things God gives often:
some he gives only once. The seasons return again and
again, and the flowers change with the months, but youth
comes twice to none." Childhood comes but once with its
opportunities. Whatever is done to stamp it with beauty
must be done quickly.

Then it matters not how capable, how wise, how
devoted the mother may be; the fact that she does her part
well does not free the father in any degree from his share of
the responsibility. Duties cannot be transferred. No other
one's faithfulness can excuse or atone for my unfaithfulness.
Besides, it is a wrong and an unmanly thing for a strong,

capable man who claims to be the stronger vessel, to seek to
put off on a woman, whom he calls the weaker vessel, duties
and responsibilities which clearly belong to himself. There
is a certain sense in which the mother is the real home-
maker. It is in her hands that the tender life is laid for its
first impressions. In all its education and culture she comes
the closer to it. Her spirit makes the home atmosphere. Yet
from end to end of the Scriptures the law of God makes the
father the head of the household, and devolves upon him as
such the responsibility for the upbuilding of his home, the
training of his children, the care of all the sacred interests
of his family.

The fathers should awake to the fact that they have
something to do in making the life of their own homes
besides providing food and clothing and paying taxes and
bills. They owe to their homes the best influences of their
lives. Whatever other duties press upon them, they should
always find time to plan for the good of their own
households. The very centre of every man's life should be
his home. Instead of being to him a mere boarding-house
where he eats and sleeps, and from which he starts out in
the mornings to his work, it ought to be the place where his
heart is anchored, where his hopes gather, to which his
thoughts turn a thousand times a day, for which he toils and
struggles, and into which he brings always the richest and
best things of his life. He should realize that he is

responsible for the character and the influence of his home-life, and that if it should fail to be what it ought to be, the blame and guilt must be upon his soul. Socrates used to say that he wondered how men who were so careful of the training of a colt were indifferent to the education of their own children. Yet even in these Christian days men are found—men professing to be followers of Christ and to believe in the superiority of life itself to all things else—who give infinitely more thought and pains to the raising of cattle, the growing of crops, the building up of business, than to the training of their children. Something must be crowded out of every earnest, busy life. No one can do everything that comes to his hand. But it will be a fatal mistake if any father allows his duties to his home to be crowded out. They should rather have the first place. Anything else had better be neglected than his children. Even religious work in the kingdom of Christ at large must not interfere with one's religious work in the kingdom of Christ in his home. No man is required by the vows and the spirit of his consecration to keep other men's vineyards so faithfully that he cannot keep his own. That a man has been a devoted pastor or a diligent church officer or a faithful Sunday-school superior teacher will not atone for the fact that he was an unfaithful father.

Definitions are important. It will help very greatly in working out the problem of the home-life to settle precisely the object of a home, and what it is intended to accomplish for those who are to grow up in it. When boys are to be trained for soldiers a military academy is what is required. If they are to serve in the navy they are sent to a naval school. The course of study, the instruction, the tone and spirit of these schools, are not the same in all, but in each are adapted to produce the end desired. If we know definitely what a home ought to do for the children who are brought up in it, we can tell better what the training, the instruction and the influences should be.

What, then, is the object of a home? What is its mission? What is it designed to accomplish? What kind of results is it expected to yield? We know the design of a blacksmith's shop; articles and implements of iron are forged and fashioned there. We know what a marble-cutter's yard is for; forms of grace and beauty are there chiseled from the block. When an artist sets up a studio we know what kind of work he expects to send out; oil canvas or in marble he will fix the beautiful creations of his genius and send them forth to give inspirations of loveliness to others. In every kind of shop or factory or mill which men build they have some definite design to accomplish, some specific results to be achieved. What are the results which homes are meant to produce? What forms of beauty, what fabrics of loveliness, are they expected to yield? We begin to think of these questions, and we say, "A home is a place in which to sleep and get one's meals. It is a place in which to rest when one is tired, to stay and be nursed when one is sick; a place in which to rock the babies and let the children romp and play; a place to receive one's friends and keep the treasures one gathers."

Is that all? Some one asked a young lady who had just completed her education, what her aim in life now was, and she replied, "To breathe." Her reply may have been made in jest, yet there are many who have no higher aim in living. And about as high an aim as most married people have in their home-making is to have as good and showy a house as they can afford, furnished in as rich style as their means will warrant, and then to live in it as comfortably as they are able, without too much exertion or self-denial.

But the true idea of a home is that it is a place for growth. It is a place for the parents themselves to grow— to grow into beauty of character, to grow in refinement, in knowledge, in strength, in wisdom, in patience, gentleness, kindliness, and all the Christian graces and virtues. It is a place for children to grow—to grow into physical vigor and health and to be trained in all that shall make them true and noble men and women. That is, just as the artist's studio is built and furnished for the definite purpose of preparing and sending out forms of beauty, so is a true home set up and all its life ordered for the definite purpose of training, building up and sending out human lives fashioned into symmetry, filled with lofty impulses and aspirations, governed by principles of rectitude and honor and fitted to enter upon the duties and struggles of life with wisdom and strength.

If this be the true object and design in setting up a home, the question arises, what sort of home-culture and home-education will produce these results? What influences will best fashion human infancy and childhood into strong, noble manhood and lovely, queenly womanhood? The smith furnishes his shop with the appliances and tools which are best fitted to do the work he intends to do. The gardener prepares his soil, sows his seeds, waters his plants, regulates the temperature and provides just the conditions adapted to promote the growth of his flowers. What sort of implements do we need in training tender lives? What are the conditions which will best promote growth in human souls? What kind of home-life must we try to make if we would build up noble character in our children?

For one thing, the house itself in which we live, with its surroundings and adornments, is important. Every home-influence, even the very smallest, works itself into the heart of childhood and then reappears in the opening character. Homes are the real schools in which men and women are trained, and fathers and mothers are the real teachers and builders of life. The poet's song that charms the world is but the sweetness of a mother's love flowing out in rhythmic measure through the soul of her child. The lovely things which men make in their days of strength are but the reproductions in embodied forms of the lovely thoughts that were whispered in their hearts in tender youth. The artist's picture is but a touch of a mother's beauty wrought out on the canvas. There is nothing in all the influences and surroundings of the home of tender childhood so small that it does not leave its touch of beauty or of marring upon the life.

Even the natural scenery in which a child is reared has much to do with the tone and hue of its future character. Beautiful things spread before the eye of childhood print themselves on the sensitive heart. The mountains, the sea, lovely valleys, picturesque landscapes, forests, flowers, all have their influence in shaping the life. Still greater is the influence of the house itself in which a child is brought up. This subject has not yet received the attention which it merits. As people advance in civilization and refinement they build better houses. In great cities the criminal and degraded classes live in wretched hovels. One of the first steps in any wise effort to elevate the low and vicious elements of society must be to provide better dwellings for them. When a whole family is crowded into one room neither physical nor moral health is possible. In a wretched, filthy apartment in a dark court or miserable alley it is impossible for children to grow up into purity and refinement.

Wherever a child grows up it carries in its character the subtle impressions of the home in which it lives. The house itself, its shape and appearance, its interior arrangement and decoration, its furnishing, its external surroundings— brick walls and paved streets or green grass and flowers—its outlook, on the majestic sea, on the grand mountains, on the illimitable prairie, on barren stretches or picturesque landscape, these have their influence on the character and help to determine its final shaping. In the choosing and preparation of a home this fact must not be overlooked. The educating power of beauty must not be forgotten. The surroundings should be cheerful and attractive. The house itself, whether large or small, should be neat and tasteful. Its ornaments and decorations should be simple yet chaste and pleasing to the eye. The rooms in which our children are to sleep and play and live we should make just as bright and lovely as our means can make them. If we can afford but two rooms for our home, we should put into them just as much educating power as possible. Children are fond of pictures, and pictures in a house, if they be pure and good, have a wondrous influence in refining their lives. In these days of cheap art, when prints and engravings can be purchased at such small cost, there is scarcely any one who may not have on the walls of his house some bright bits of beauty which will prove an inspiration to his children. Every home can at least be made bright, clean, sweet, and beautiful, even if bare of ornament and decoration. It is almost impossible for a child to grow up into loveliness of character, gentleness of disposition and purity of heart amid scenes of slovenliness, untidiness, repulsiveness and filthiness. But a home clean, tasteful, with simple adornments and pleasant surprises is an influence of incalculable value in the education of children.

But the house is not all. Four walls do not make a home, though built of marble and covered with rarest decorations. A family may be reared in a palace filled with the loveliest works of art, and yet the influences may not be such as leave blessing. The home-life itself is more important than the house and its adornments. By the home-life is meant all the intercourse of the members of the family. It is a happy art, the art of living together in tender love. It must begin with the parents themselves. Unless their life together is loving and true it will be impossible for them to make their home-life so. They give the keynote to the music. If their intercourse is marked by bickering and quarreling they must expect their children to imitate them. If gentleness and affectionateness characterize their bearing toward each other the same spirit will rule in the family life. For their children's sake, if for no other, parents should cultivate their own lives and train themselves to live together in the most Christlike way. They will very soon learn that good rules and wise counsel from their lips amount to but little unless their own lives give example and illustration of the things thus commended.

We enter some homes, and they are full of sweetness as summer fields are of fragrance. All is order, beauty, gentleness and peace. We enter other homes, where we find jarring, selfishness, harshness and disorder. This difference is not accidental. There are influences at work in each home which yield just the result we see in each. There are different kinds of shells in the sea. Some of them are very coarse, ugly and unsightly; others are very lovely, like the nautilus, "many chambered, softly curved, pearl-adorned, glowing with imprisoned rainbows." But each shell exactly corresponds with the nature of the creature that lives in it. Each little creature builds a house just like itself; indeed it builds its own life into it. In like manner every home takes its color and tone from its makers. A refined spirit puts refinement into a home, though it be only one plain room without an ornament or a luxury; a coarse nature makes the home coarse, though it be a palace filled with all the elegances that wealth can buy. No home-life can ever be better than the life of those who make it. It is nothing less nor more than the spirit of the parents like an atmosphere filling all the house.

What should this home-spirit be? First of all, I would

name the law of *unselfishness* as one of its essential elements. Where selfishness prevails there can be no real happiness. Indeed there is no deep, true and holy love where selfishness rules. As love grows, selfishness dies out in the heart. Love is always ready to deny itself, to give, to sacrifice, just in the measure of its sincerity and intensity. Perfect love is perfect self-forgetfulness. Hence, where there is love in a home, unselfishness is the law. Each forgets self and lives for the others. But when there is selfishness it mars the joy. One selfish soul will destroy the sweetness of the life of any home. It is like an ugly thorn-bush in the midst of a garden of flowers.

It was selfishness that destroyed the first home and blighted all the loveliness of Paradise; and it has been blighting lovely things in earth's homes ever since. We need to guard against this spirit. Selfishness in parents will spread the same unhappy spirit through all the household life. They must be, not in seeming but in reality, what they want their children to be. The lessons they would teach they must live.

Another essential element of true home-life is *affectionateness*; not love only, but the cultivation of love in the daily life of the family, the expression of love in words and acts. This reminder is not altogether needless. There are homes where the love is deep and true; the members of the family would die for each other; when grief or pain comes to one of them the hearts of all the others give out their warmest expressions of affection. There is no question as to the reality and strength of the attachment that binds the household together. Yet in their ordinary intercourse there is a great lack of those exhibitions of kindly feeling which are the sweetest blossomings of love. Husband and wife pass weeks without one of those endearing expressions which have such power to warm the heart. Meals are eaten in haste and in dreary silence, as if the company that surround the table had nothing in common and had only been brought together by accident. The simplest courtesies that even polite strangers never fail to extend to each other are altogether omitted in the household intercourse. Ill manners that would not be tolerated for a moment in the ordinary associations of society are oftentimes allowed to find their way into this holiest circle.

This should not be so. The heart's love should be permitted to flow out in word and deed. There are such homes. The very atmosphere as one enters the door seems laden with fragrance. The conversation is bright, sparkling, cheerful, courteous. The warmth of love makes itself felt in continuous influence. No loud, harsh tones are ever heard. A delightful thoughtfulness pervades all the family life. Every one is watchful of the feelings of the others. There is a respectfulness of manner and bearing that is shown even toward the youngest, toward servants. Without any such sickening extravagances of expression as mark the intercourse of some families, there is here a genuine kindliness of manner which is very charming even to the casual visitor, and which for the hearts of the household has a wondrous warming and satisfying power. All the amenities and courtesies of true politeness are carefully observed, touched also by a tenderness which shows that they are from the heart.

This is the true home spirit. It needs culture. Even the best of us are in danger of growing careless in our own family life. Our very familiarity with our home companions is apt to render us forgetful, and when we have grown forgetful and have dropped the little tendernesses out of our home intercourse, soon the love itself will begin to decay, and what the end may be of coldness and desolateness no one can foretell.

The home-life should also be made bright and full of sunshine. The courtesy of the true home is not stiff and formal but sincere, simple and natural. Children need an atmosphere of gladness. Law should not make its restraints hang like chains upon them. Sternness and coldness should have no place in home-life or in family government. No child can ever grow up into its richest and best development in a home which is gloomy and unhappy. No more do plants need sunshine and air than children need joy and gladness. Unhappiness stunts them, so that their sweetest graces never come out.

Some one says: "Make your children happy in their youth; let distinction come to them, if it will, after well-spent and well-remembered years." Wise parents will see that their home possesses the essential conditions of happiness. They will sympathize with their children and take care never to grow away from them in spirit, though carrying the weightiest responsibilities or wearing the highest honors among men. The busiest father should find at least a few moments every day to romp with his children. A man who is too stately and dignified to play with his baby or carry his little ones or help them in their sports and games, not only lacks one of the finest elements of true greatness, but fails in one of his duties to his children. In no other way can he so enshrine himself in their hearts as by giving them daily a few precious moments of gladness associated with himself which shall endear him to them for ever. No father can afford to let his children grow up without weaving himself into the memories of their golden youth.

Norman McLeod says: "Oh sunshine of youth, let it shine on! Let love flow out fresh and full, unchecked by any rule but what love creates, and pour itself down without stint into the young heart. Make the days of boyhood happy; for other days of labor and sorrow must come, when the blessing of those dear eyes and clasping hands and sweet

caressings will, next to the love of God from whence they
flow, save the wall from losing faith in the human heart, help
to deliver him from the curse of selfishness, and be all Eden
in the evening when life is driven forth into the wilderness
of life." Another writes: "The richest heritage that parents
can give is a happy childhood, with tender memories of
father and mother. This will brighten the coming days when
the children have gone out from the sheltering home, and
will be a safeguard in times of temptation and a conscious
help amid the stern realities of life."

Whatever parents may do for their children, they
should at least make their childhood sunny and tender.
Their young lives are so delicate that harshness may mar
their beauty for ever, and so sensitive that every influence
that falls upon them leaves its trace, which grows into the
character either as a grace or a blemish. A happy childhood
stores away sunshine in the chambers of the heart which
brightens the life to its close. An unhappy childhood may so
fill the life's fountains with bitterness as to sadden all the
after years.

"Wait not till the little hands are at rest
Ere you fill them full of flowers;
Wait not for the crowning tuberose
To make sweet life last sad hours
But while, in life busy household band,

Your darlings still need your guiding hand,
Oh fill their lives with sweetness.

Remember the homes whence the light has fled,
Where the rose has faded away;
And the love that glows in youthful hearts,
Oh, cherish it while you may,
And make your home a garden of flowers,
Where joy shall bloom through childhood's hours,
And fill young lives with sweetness."

Something must be said concerning the training of children. It is to be kept in mind that the object of the home is to build up manhood and womanhood. This work of training belongs to the parents and cannot be transferred. It is a most delicate and responsible duty, one from which a thoughtful soul would shrink with awe and fear were it not for the assurance of divine help. Yet there are many parents who do not stop to think of the responsibility which is laid upon them when a little child enters their home.

Look at it a moment. What is so feeble, so helpless, so dependent as a new-born babe? Yet look onward and see what a stretch of life lies before this feeble infant, away into the eternities. Think of the powers folded up in this helpless form, and what the possible outcome may be. Who can tell what skill there may be lying unconscious yet in these tiny fingers, what eloquence or song in these little lips, what intellectual faculties in this brain, what power of love or sympathy in this heart? The parents are to take this infant and nurse it into manhood or womanhood, to draw out these slumbering powers and teach it to use them. That is, God wants a man trained for a great mission in the world, and life puts into the hands of a young father and mother a little babe, and bids them nurse it and train it for him until the man is ready for his mission; or at least to have sole charge of his earliest years when the first impressions must be made, which shall mould and shape his whole career.

When we look at a little child and remember all this, what a dignity surrounds the work of caring for it! Does God give to angels any work grander than this?

Women sigh for fame. They would be sculptors, and chisel out of the cold stone forms of beauty to fill the world with admiration of their skill. Or they would be poets, to write songs to thrill a nation and to be sung around the world. But is any work in marble so great as hers who has an immortal life laid in her hands to shape for its destiny? Is the writing of any poem in musical lines so noble a work as the training of the powers of a human soul into harmony? Yet there are women who regard the duties and cares of motherhood as too obscure and commonplace tasks for their hands. So when a baby comes a nurse is hired, who for a weekly compensation agrees to take charge of the little one, that the mother may be free from such drudgery to devote herself to the nobler and worthier things that she finds to do.

Is the following indictment too strong? "A mother will secure from the nearest intelligence-office a girl who undertakes to relieve her of the charge of her little one, and will hand over to this mere hireling, this ignorant stranger, the soul-mothering which God has entrusted to her. She has mothered the body—any one will do to mother the soul. So the little one is left in the hands of this hireling, placed under her constant influence, subjected to the subtle impress of her spirit, to draw into its inner being the life, be it what it may, of this uncultured soul. She wakens its first thoughts, rouses its earliest emotions, brings the delicate action of motives to bear upon the will—generally in such hands a compound force of bullying and bribing, mean fear and mean desire—tends it, plays with it, lives with it; and thus the young mother is free to dress and drive, to visit and receive, to enjoy balls and operas, discharging her trust for an immortal life by proxy! Is there any malfeasance in office, in these days of dishonor, like unto this? Our women crowd the churches to draw the inspiration of religion for their daily duties, and then prove recreant to the first of all fidelities, the most solemn of all responsibilities. We hear fashionable young mothers boast that they are not tied down to their nurseries, but are free to keep in the old gay life; as though there was no shame to the soul of womanhood therein."

Oh that God would give every mother a vision of the glory and splendor of the work that is given to her when a babe is placed in her bosom to be nursed and trained! Could she have but one glimpse into the future of that life as it reaches on into eternity; could she look into its soul to see its possibilities; could she be made to understand her own personal responsibility for the training of this child, for the development of its life, and for its destiny,—she would see that in all God's world there is no other work so noble and so worthy of her best powers, and she would commit to no other hands the sacred and holy trust given to her.

This is not the place to present theories of family government; I am trying only to define the parents' part in making the home. So far as their children are concerned, their part is to train them for life, to send them out of the home ready for whatever duty or mission God may have ready for them. Only this much may be said—whatever may be alone in the way of governing, teaching or training, theories are not half so important as the parents' lives. They may teach the most beautiful things, but if the child does not see these things in the life of them he will not consider them important enough to be adopted in his own life. To quote here the words of another: "You cannot give your child what you do not possess: you can scarcely help giving your child what you do possess. If you are a coward you cannot make him brave; if he becomes brave it will be in spite of you. If you are a deceiver you cannot make him truthful; if you are selfish you cannot make him generous; if you are self-willed you cannot make him yielding; if you are passionate you cannot make him temperate and self-controlled. The parent's life flows into the child's life. We impress ourselves upon our children less by what we teach them than by what we are. Your child is a sensitive plate; you are sitting before the camera; if you do not like the picture the fault is with yourself. One angry word from your lips will outweigh a hundred rebukes of anger. One selfish deed, one social deception, will do more to mar than a hundred homilies can do to make."

What we want to do with our children is not merely to control them and keep them in order, but to implant true principles deep in their hearts which shall rule their whole lives; to shape their character from within into Christlike beauty, and to make of them noble men and women, strong for battle and for duty. They are to be trained rather than governed. Growth of character, not merely good behavior, is the object of all home governing and teaching. Therefore the home influence is far more important than the home laws, and the parents' lives are of more moment than their teachings.

Men say that into the strings of some old Cremona

violin the life of the master who once played upon it has passed, so that it is as an impersonal soul, breathing out at every skillful touch. This is only a beautiful poetic fancy. But when a little child in a mother's bosom is loved, nursed, caressed, held close to her heart, prayed over, wept over, talked with, for days, weeks, months, years, it is no mere fancy to say that the mother's life has indeed passed into the child's soul. What it becomes is determined by what the mother is. The early years settle what its character will be, and these are the mother's years.

O mothers of young children, I bow before you in reverence. Your work is most holy. You are fashioning the destinies of immortal souls. The powers folded up in the little ones that you hushed to sleep in your bosoms last night are powers that shall exist for ever. You are preparing them for their immortal destiny and influence. Be faithful. Take up your sacred burden reverently. Be sure that your heart is pure and that your life is sweet and clean. The Persian apologue says that the lump of clay was fragrant because it had lain on a rose. Let your life be as the rose, and then your child as it lies upon your bosom will absorb the fragrance. If there is no sweetness in the rose the clay will not be perfumed.

History is full of illustrations of the power of parental influence. It either brightens or darkens the child's life to the close. It is either a benediction which makes every day better and happier, or it is a curse which leaves blight and sorrow on every hour. Thousands have been saved from drifting away by the holy memories of happy, godly homes, or, when they have drifted away, have been drawn back by the same charm of power. There are no chains so strong as the cords that a true home throws about the heart. John Randolph said, "I used to be called a Frenchman because I took the French side in politics. But though this is false, I should have been a French atheist, had it not been for one recollection, and that was the memory of the time when my now departed mother used to take my little hands in hers, and, causing me to bow at her knee, taught me to pray 'Our Father who art in heaven.'" Is it not worth while for parents to seek to have such abiding, strong and blessed influence over their children's lives? Just as far-reaching and as powerful is the evil influence if parents are unholy. When the morning sun rises the shadow of Mount Etna is cast far across the lovely island of Sicily, resting on gardens and fields and the people's homes, a shadow always of gloom, a shadow as of an ever-imminent terror. So over the life of a child to its close hangs the shadow of an ungodly parental influence. What parent wants to project such fatal gloom over the future years of the child he loves so well?

When I think of the sacredness and the responsibility of parents, I do not see how any father and mother can look upon the little child that has been given to them and consider their duty to it, and not be driven to God by the very weight of the burden that rests upon them, to cry to him for help and wisdom. When an impenitent man bends over the cradle of his first-born, when he begins to realize that here is a soul which he must train, teach, fashion and guide through this world to God's bar how can he longer stay away from God? Let him, as he bends over his child's crib to kiss its sweet lips, ask himself: "Am I true to my child while I shut God out of my own life? Am I able to meet this solemn responsibility of parenthood all alone, in my unaided human weakness, without divine help?" I know not how any father can honestly meet these questions as he looks upon his innocent, helpless child, given to him to shelter, to keep, to guide, and not fall instantly upon his knees and give himself to God. Rather would I see my own little ones laid away in the grave to-morrow, and miss from my life henceforth all their love, and go with empty arms and sobbing heart through this world to life's close, than to attempt to train them, teach them and lead them on without the help of God.

"Better be out on the boundless sea, without knowledge of the stars above or the currents beneath; better be in the untrodden forest without pathway or compass; better be on the trackless desert without a landmark in all the horizon, nothing but burning sand under foot and brazen sky over head, than to be on this sea, in this wilderness, upon this desert of our life, with a human destiny entrusted to your care and no guiding God to pilot you to him and the desired haven! But with God's presence, help and guidance even this great and responsible work shall not crush you nor make you afraid."

There is an old picture which represents a woman who has fallen asleep at her wheel, in very weariness, as she toils to fulfill her household duties, and the angels have come and are softly finishing her task while she sleeps. Let parents be faithful; let them do their best. The work may seem too great for them, and they may faint under its burdens and seem to fail. But what they cannot do the angels will come and finish while they sleep. Night by night they will come and correct the day's mistakes, and if need be do all the poor, faulty work over again. Then at last when the parents sleep in death, dropping out of their hands the sacred work they have been doing for their children, again God's angels will come, take up the unfinished work and carry it on to completeness.

THE CHILDREN'S PART

What would I not give," said Charles Lamb, "to call my dear mother back to earth for a single day, to ask her pardon, upon my knees, for all those acts by which I grieved her gentle spirit!"

Many another sensitive heart has felt the same pain when standing by a parent's grave, and has sighed in like manner for an opportunity to speak its penitence and its cries for pardon into the dead ear. But filial love blossoms out too late when it waits till the parental ear is beyond the reach of human cry. The time for the child to show his affection and gratitude is along the years, while the father and mother are living and treading earth's paths. If he then strews thorns for their feet, what does it avail that he brings flowers for their burial? If he dishonors them by disobedience, by unkindness, by unworthy conduct, by sin, what does it avail that he sets up the costly monuments over their graves, cutting in the white marble his praises of their virtues and their faithfulness?

The place for the flowers is along the hard paths of toil and care and burden-bearing. The best monument for grateful affection to erect is a noble, beautiful life, a joy to the heart and an honor in the eyes of fond parental hope. Kindness to the living is better than bitter tears of penitence over the dead.

The debt of children to a true home is one that never can be overpaid, or even fully discharged. It dates from the first moment of their being; it accumulates as the days and years pass on. There are the years of helpless infancy with their solicitations, their broken nights and toilsome days, their unsleeping thoughtfulness and unselfish sacrifice, their gentle nursing and patient watching. There are the years of training and teaching, when the bodily powers are being developed, the feet taught to walk, the hands to handle, the tongue to speak, when the mental faculties are being drawn out, and when all the functions of life are being trained to their several uses. There are the times of sickness when the lamp never goes out in the room by night, and the pale, weary watcher accepts no relief till the danger is past. There are long years of anxieties, of prayers, of tears, of hopes, of disappointments, of sacrifices, of pains and toils. The best that a child can do for true parents will never repay them for what they have done for him.

The question, therefore, "What is the children's part in the home-life?" is no unimportant one. They have a place in making the home joyful. Dreary is the household life where no children ever come; very lonely and desolate is the home where they come and stay for a time and then go away. Unconsciously, the children have a most sacred and holy part in the home life from their earliest infancy. Then all along their years, while they remain under the old home-roof and after they leave its shelter to set up homes of their own, they have duties to perform and obligations to render to those who gave them birth and watched over their helpless years.

The little wheels of a watch do not seem to be important; yet if one of them is broken, or if it is bent, or if it fails to perform its part, all the wheels will be arrested in their motion and the watch will stop. If the smallest wheel goes wrong, moves too fast or too slow, the hands on the dial likewise go wrong. There is no part of the delicate machinery of the watch so small that it makes no difference how it does its duty.

When the question is asked, "What part have the children in making the home-life?" some one may answer, "The children cannot do anything, at least while they are small to aid in making the home what it should be. They cannot help make money to buy bread. They cannot do the work. When they grow older they can be of use, but when they are young all they can do is to be rocked and petted while they are babies, and then as they grow larger go to school and eat and romp and wear out clothes. They cannot help in any way; they are only burdens."

But wait a minute. They are not so useless, after all. They are like the tiny wheels of the watch. They may not look large enough to be of any use, and yet there is not a child in any true home so small as to have no influence. There is not even a baby that does not unconsciously affect all the home-life by its coming. Indeed, every baby is an emperor, with crown and sceptre, and from its throne on the mother's bosom it rules all the house. The father, out at his work in the busy world, has a lighter, warmer heart because he is thinking of the baby at home. The mother gets through all her work more easily because her baby is sleeping in its crib or kicking up its heels on the floor beside her. The boys and girls are gentler, more quiet and more thoughtful since Baby came. No one can say that any child is too small to have a part in making the home-life. Of course a baby's part is done unconsciously, and it is not to be held to responsibility as are the children who have grown older. This chapter is not addressed to babies, but to those who are of sufficient age to know what they ought to do and to try to do it.

Here is the question on which every child, living in a parent's house, should think much: "What is my part in making this home what it should be?"

You know what a true home ought to be. It ought to be a place where love rules. It ought to be beautiful, bright, joyous, full of tenderness and affection; a place in which all are growing happier and better each day. There should never be any discord, any wrangling, any angry words or bitter feelings. The home-life should be a harmonious song without one jarring note, day after day. The home, no matter how humble it is, how plain, how small, should be the dearest spot on the earth to each member of the family. It should be made so happy a place and so full of love that no matter where one may wander in after years, in any of the ends of the earth, his home should still hold its invisible lines of influence about him, and should ever draw resistlessly upon his heart. It ought to be the one spot in all the earth to which he would turn first in trouble or in danger. It should be the refuge of his soul in every trial and grief.

To make a home such a power in one's after life it must be happy in the days of childhood and youth. Have childhood and youth any responsibility for the realizing of this ideal of home? Is it altogether and only the parents' work? So far as infancy is concerned there certainly is no responsibility. The father and mother must do all, and the little one is only a tender and lovely plant growing in the garden which parental hands tend. But with the years of consciousness comes responsibility, and then every child helps either to make or mar the home's blessedness and the home's joy.

What should the child-life be that would perfectly

fulfill its part in the home? We have a model. Once there was a home on earth in which a Child lived whose life was spotless and faultless, and who realized all that is lovely, tender and true in child-life. If we only knew how Jesus lived as a child in that Nazareth home it would help other children to live aright. We know that he helped to make the home happy. He never caused his parents one anxiety, one pang, one moment of shame. He never failed in a duty. We know that he did his part well in the making of that home and if we only had a memoir of his years of childhood telling us what he did, every other child could study it and imitate his example.

We have no such memoir, but we have one single glimpse into his home-life which reveals a great deal. We see him at twelve years of age. He is in the temple at Jerusalem. He has been lost from his parents in the great caravan returning from the passover, and when they find him again we are told in one brief sentence that he went down with them to Nazareth, and was subject unto them. Then for eighteen years longer he remained in that home; we have not another word about him; not another glimpse do we get of him or of his home; Scripture is silent concerning him all those years. We have only this one sentence about the way in which he lived in that home: "He went down with them to Nazareth, and was subject unto them." Yet this one glimpse really reveals the whole history of those years. He was subject to his parents.

Remember who this Child was. It was over his birth that the angels sang their song: "Glory to God in the highest; on earth peace, good will to men." He was the eternal Son of God. He had made all the worlds. He had adorned the heavens. Him all the hosts of glory obeyed. Yet he humbled himself, veiled his glory, and dwelt in a lowly home of earth for thirty years. He submitted himself to earthly parents and obeyed them. Then he wrought himself with his own hands to help support the home. No details are given—just this one word; but we can easily fill out the picture for ourselves. We see, for thirty years, from infancy to full manhood, this holy Child exhibiting toward his parents the most perfect dutifulness, obedience, honor and helpfulness. He obeyed them, not by constraint, but cheerfully, all these years. He did his part well in the making of that home.

This example is the answer to the question of this chapter; and what is it but this, that the great duty of childhood in the home-life is *to obey*? He was subject unto them. Although he was the Son of God, yet he learned obedience to human parents. He did their will and not his own. He had entered upon the affairs of his heavenly Father. In the temple he had said, "Wist ye not that I must be about my Father's business?" (The Revised Version renders it "in my Father's house," but gives in the margin as

the literal rendering "in the things of my Father." Alford
says: "Primarily in the house of my Father; but we must not
exclude the wider sense, which embraces all places and
employments of my Father's.")

Yet immediately after saying this he went back to his
own home to take and keep for eighteen years more the
place of a child. Hence we conclude that the Father's
business for him all those years was subjection to his earthly
parents. That was the work which was given him to do for
that time. He had come to the earth on a great mission, the
greatest ever undertaken or performed in the universe, yet
the place in which he was prepared for that mission was not
in any of the fine schools of the world, but in a lowly home;
not at the feet of rabbis and philosophers, but with his own
mother for his teacher. What an honor does this fact put
upon home! What a dignity upon motherhood!

It would seem that no argument after that were needed
to prove to children the duty and the dignity of obedience
to parents. We take our place far back in the history of the
world; we stand under the cloud-crowned, fire-wreathed
Sinai, and amidst its awful thunderings we hear the voice of
God proclaim: "Honor thy father and thy mother; that thy
days may be long upon the land which the Lord thy God
giveth thee." But even all these scenes of majesty—the voice
of Jehovah, the burning mountain, the cloud and the
thunder—did not give to this command such sacred

authority, such solemn importance, as when Jesus, the Son of God, for thirty years in a lowly home on earth, submitted himself to human parents and obeyed their commands.

Does any question ever arise as to the authority of this divine word in the Decalogue? This picture of Jesus obeying it in that Galilean home is sufficient answer.

Does the thought ever arise, "Is it manly—is it womanly—to yield to my parents, to have no will of my own, to do their bidding in all things?" Behold Jesus till thirty years of age yielding to the control of his human parents, asking them continually what they would have him to do, referring every question to them. Was it manly in him? Surely then it cannot be unmanly in any son of earthly parents in this world. Where shall we learn manliness if not in the life and from the example of Jesus? Thomas Hughes says, in speaking of manliness and of courage as one of its elements:

"Tenacity of will lies at the root of all courage, but courage can only rise into true manliness when the will is surrendered; and the more absolute the surrender of the will the more perfect will be the temper of our courage and the strength of our manliness." There is nothing manlier in all Christ's life than his quiet subjection to his parents in that cottage at Nazareth, though conscious of his divine origin and nature and of his glorious mission. There is no manlier thing ever seen on this earth than a man in the prime of his strength and power showing deference and love to a humble parent and yielding obedience and honor as if he were a little child.

Does some evil spirit suggest that such subjection to parents keeps one down, puts chains on his freedom, keeps him under restraint and hinders him from rising into grandeur and nobleness of character? Did it have such effect on Jesus? Did the thirty years of submission in his home cramp and fetter his manhood? Did his subjection break his power, repress the glorious aspiration of his soul, stunt and hinder the development of his life and make his career a failure in the end? We know well that it did not. There was a preparation for his mission which, as a man, he could have gotten in no other way but by the discipline he obtained in his own home. No human powers were ever yet cramped or stunted or repressed by taking the place of subjection in a true home. Rather, that life will always be more or less a failure which in its earlier years does not learn to submit and be ruled. No one is fitted for ruling others who has not first learned in his place to obey.

Some one may say again: "My parents are very plain people. They have never known much of the world. They have missed the opportunities that I am enjoying, and therefore have not intelligence or wisdom or education sufficient to direct my life."

We have only to remember again who Jesus was. Was

there ever any human parent in this world who was really worthy or capable, in this sense, to be his teacher, to guide and control his life? Was there ever, in any home on earth, such a distance between parents and child as there was in that home at Nazareth? Yet this Son of God, with all his wisdom, his knowledge, his grandeur of character, did not hesitate to submit himself to the training of that peasant mother and that peasant father. Shall any other child, in view of this model child-life at home, assert that he is too far advanced, too much superior in knowledge and culture, too wise and intelligent, to submit to the parents God has given him? If Christ could be taught and trained by his lowly parents for his glorious mission, where is the true parent who is not worthy to be his own child's guide and teacher?

This, then, is the part of every child in the home-life. This is the way in which children can do the most to make the home true and happy. It is the part of the parents to guide, to train, to teach, to mould the character. God holds them responsible for this. They must qualify themselves to do it. Then it is the part of the children to accept this guidance, teaching, training and shaping at the parents' hands. When both faithfully do their part the home-life will be a sweet song of love; where either fails there will be discordant life, and the angel of blessing will not leave his benison of peace.

Such, in general, is the central feature of the children's

part in the home-life: to recognize their parents as the head and to yield to them in all things. This is not meant to make them slaves. The home-life I am depicting is ruled by love; the parental authority is exercised in love; it seeks only the highest good of each child; it asks nothing unreasonable or unjust. If it withholds things that a child desires, it is either because it is not able to grant them or because the granting of them would work injury rather than benefit. If it seeks to guide the tender feet in a way that is not the chosen way, nor the most easy and pleasant way, it is because a riper wisdom sees that it is the best way. True parental guidance is love grown wise. It is an imitation of God's government. He is our Father and we are his children. We are to obey him absolutely and without question. Yet it is no blind obedience. We know that he loves us with a love deep, tender, unchanging. We know that he is wiser than we, infinitely wiser, and can never err. We know that when he denies a request the granting of it would be an unkindness; when he leads us in another path than the one we had marked out, his is the right way; when he chastens or corrects there is love in his chastisement or correction. We know that in all his government and discipline he is seeking only our highest good. Our whole duty therefore as God's children is to yield ourselves to his will. True human parenthood is a faint copy of the divine, and to its direction and guidance children are to submit.

This subjection implies obedience to the commands of parents. Thus Paul interprets it: "Children, obey your parents in the Lord; for this is right;" and again, "Children, obey your parents in all things; for this is well-pleasing unto the Lord." It is right on moral grounds, and this ought to settle the matter. True manliness never wants to know more than that a thing is right, is duty. Devotion to duty, at whatever cost, is one of the first elements of heroism. It is right that children should obey their parents, and no further question need be asked, no further reason for obeying need be sought.

But it is also well-pleasing unto the Lord. He is watching how every child acts, and he is well pleased when he sees obedience. This ought to furnish an additional motive, if any were needed. The thought that doing a certain duty faithfully muses emotions of pleasure and approval in the heart of God certainly ought to be a wonderful spur and incentive to heroic fidelity.

This obedience is to extend to "all things," the things that are agreeable and the things that are disagreeable. Though he may be unjustly treated the child is not to rebel. He may know that his parent is unkind or oppressive, or even cruel, but his duty is not thereby changed. Wrong on the parent's part will never justify wrong on the part of the child. There is only one qualification: children are to obey their parents "in the Lord." If the parent commands the child to commit a sin, of course he is not to obey. Herodias was under no moral obligation to obey when her cruel and bloody mother bade her ask for the head of John the Baptist. No human authority is ever binding when it bids us break a divine law. No true parent will knowingly ask anything of his child that is not right; hence the law of parental government requires obedience in all things.

It is told of General Havelock that one day, when a boy, his father, having some business to do, left him on London bridge and bade him wait there till he came back. The father was detained and forgot his son, not returning to the bridge all the day. In the evening he reached home, and after he had rested a little while his wife inquired: "Where's Harry?" The father thought a moment. "Dear me!" said he, "I quite forgot Harry. He is on London bridge, and has been there for eight hours waiting for me." He hastened away to relieve the boy, and found him just where he had left him in the morning, pacing to and fro like a sentinel on his beat. That father knew just where to find his son because he knew that he always obeyed his commands. It is such obedience that pleases God, while it ensures harmony and peace in the home. The parents are the divinely constituted head of the family, and it is the children's part to obey.

This requirement implies also *honor and respect*. "Honor thy father and thy mother," says the command. Honor is a larger word than obey. We may obey a person whom we do not respect. We are to honor our parents—that is, reverence them—as well as obey them.

There is no need for any argument to prove that every child should honor his parents. Yet it is idle to deny that there is on every hand a lack of filial respect. There are many children who show by their words or acts that their parents are not sacredly enshrined in their hearts.

I heard a bright young girl, well dressed, with good manners and good face, say that her mother looked so old-fashioned that she was ashamed to have her in the parlor or to walk with her on the street. I chanced to know a little about that mother and that daughter. I knew that one reason why the mother looked so old-fashioned, and probably lacked something of refinement of manner, was because of her devotion to the interests of her daughter; she had made a sacrifice of herself for her daughter's sake; she had denied herself in dress and ornament that her daughter might appear well and be admired.

Some young people may read these pages who at times feel as this young lady did. Have you ever sat down quietly to think over and sum up the debt you owe to your old-fashioned mother? Look at the matter for a few moments. Begin with the time when you were a very little baby, as you certainly were once, however great you are now, and think what she had to do for you then. She had to nurse you hour after hour and be awake many a night to take care of you.

Sometimes you were very cross, though you are so gentle now; yet, no matter how cross you were, she was as patient as an angel with you. She wore herself out for you then.

As you grew older she taught you. Did you ever think how little you knew when you came into this world? You had hands and feet and eyes and tongue and brain, but you did not know what they were for or how to use them. It was your loving, patient mother who taught you to walk and to talk and to look and to think.

You have been a great deal of trouble to your mother in your time but she has borne it all cheerfully that you might have what you wanted. She has worked very hard that you might receive an education and be fitted to shine in society among your friends and be ready for an honored and useful place in this world.

Sometimes you think she looks very plain and old-fashioned. Perhaps she does; perhaps she is more than a little faded and worn; but did you ever think that it is because she has given so much of the best power and energy of her life to caring for you? If she had not chosen to toil and suffer and deny herself for your sake, if she had thought more of herself and less of you, she might have been very much fairer and fresher now. If she had only neglected you instead of herself she might shine now with you in the parlor, for once her cheeks were as lovely as yours are now. She might have found more rest and less hard work if she had not chosen to spend so many hours in stitching away on frocks, trowsers, jackets or dresses for you, making new and mending the old. She might have better clothes even now to wear, so that you would not blush to have your friends meet her with you, if she did not take much interest in dressing you prettily and richly. It may be that the little allowance of money that she gets is not sufficient to dress both herself and you in fashionable array, and that you may be well-clad she wears the same dress and bonnet year after year.

Never forget where your mother lost her freshness and youthful beauty—it was in self-denying toil and suffering for your sake. Those wrinkles in her face, those deep care-lines in her cheeks, that weary look in her eye, she wears all these marks now where once there was fresh beauty because she has forgotten herself these long years in loving devotion to you. These scars of time and toil and pain are the seals of her care for you.

Look at your father too. He is not so fresh and youthful as he once was. Perhaps he does not dress so finely as some of the young people you see about you or as their fathers dress. There are marks of hard toil upon him, marks of care and anxiety, which in your eye seem to disfigure his beauty. It may be that you blush a little sometimes when your young friends meet you walking with him or when he comes into the parlor when you have company, and wish he would take more pains to appear well. Do not forget that he is toiling these days for you and that his hard hands and his bronzed face are really tokens of his love for you. If he does not appear quite so fresh and handsome as some other men very likely it is because he has to work harder to give you your pleasant home, your good clothes, your daily food and many comforts, and to send you to school. When you look at him and feel tempted to be ashamed of his appearance just remember this.

Perhaps he is now an old man, with bent form, white hair, slow step, awkward hand, wrinkled face and feeble, broken voice. Forget not what history there is in all these marks that look to you like marrings of his manly beauty. The soul writes its story on the body. The soldier's scars tell of heroisms and sacrifices. The merchant's anxious face and knit brow tell of struggle and anxiety. So gluttony and greed and selfishness and licentiousness write out their record in unmistakable lines on the features, and so do kindness, benevolences, unselfishness, and purity. You look at your father and see signs of toil, of pain, of self-denial, of care. Do you know what they reveal? They tell the story of his life. He has passed through struggles and conflicts. Do you know how much of this story, if rightly interpreted, concerns you? Is there nothing in the beat form, the faded hands, the lines of care, that tells you of his deep love for you and of sufferings endured, sacrifices made and toils and anxieties for your sake?

When you think thus of what you owe your parents and of what they have borne and wrought for you, can you ever again be ashamed of them? Will not the shame rather be for yourself that you could ever have been so ungrateful as to blush at their homeliness? All the reverence of your soul will be kindled into deepest, purest admiration as you look upon these marks of love and sacrifice for your sake. You will honor them all the more, the more they are worn and wasted, the more they are broken and their grace and beauty shattered. These tokens of self-neglect and self-sacrifice are the jewels in the crown of love.

This honor is not to be shown only by the young child living yet as a child in the old home, but by those who are grown up to full manhood and womanhood. While parents live there never comes a time when a child is no longer a child, owing love and honor. Few things in this world are so beautiful as the sight of a middle-aged man or woman showing true devotion to an aged father or mother. In all the story of the life of President Garfield there is no one incident that will be longer or more tenderly remembered than that little scene on the day of his inauguration, in which he showed such honor to his aged mother. When the last words were spoken and the ceremony was ended; when he was now President of this great nation, and while the huzzas of the vast throngs were falling upon his ear, and when the greatest and noblest of the land were pressing forward to speak their applause, he turned away from all this, from the cheers of a nation, from the salutations of the great, from the congratulations of foreign ambassadors who bore messages from kings and queens, to give the first thought of that supreme hour to a little aged and worn woman who sat behind him, encircling her with his strong arm and kissing her. It was she to whom he owed all that he was. In the days of poverty she had toiled and suffered for him. She had been both father and mother to him. She had struggled with adversity and had never spared herself that she might bless his early years. She was plain and poor and wrinkled and unfashionable, but she was his mother and in that hour his loyal, manly heart honored her above all the world. President Garfield will be honored himself in all the future of our country; honored for his noble character and his kingly rank among men; honored for his achievements in the days of war and in the days of peace; honored for the splendor of soul that shone out from his sick-room in those long, weary days of death-struggle; but in all the brilliant glory that flashes about his name no one record will shine more imperishably than the sentence that tells how in the moment of his supremest exaltation he bent and printed a kiss of recognition and honor on the wasted face of his mother.

His is not the only case. This noble trait is not so rare as we might think, though it sometimes shines with a lustre

so brilliant as to draw all eyes to itself. Life's history is not
all written. Love's noble deeds are not all wrought in the
eyes of the world. Much of the rarest and noblest heroism
of love is never seen by human eyes. There are other great
men who have shown the same reverence and love for
parents in age or feebleness. There are noble daughters too
who forego the joys offered to them in homes of their own,
refusing offers of marriage and voluntarily choosing to live
without its blessing and comfort that they may shelter in
old age and surround with love's tenderness the father or
the mother or both, who filled their youth with sunshine.
Here and there a heroism finds its way into record; but the
noblest heroisms of life, the tenderest histories of love, the
most sacred things wrought by human affection remain
unwritten and untold.

Men talk of the wickedness of this world, and surely it
is wicked enough. Sin leaves blackness everywhere. There
are horrors of ingratitude, of meanness, of shame of guilt,
which make earth a stench in God's nostrils. Yet amid all
that is so revolting there are records of such sacred
tenderness, such holy beauty, such ineffable love that angels
must pause over them in reverence. These are fragments of
the Eden loveliness that float down upon the dark tide, like
lilies pure and white and unsullied on the black waters of
some stagnant bog. In earth's homes where the story of
Christ's love has been told, there are filial devotions that are

as fair as angelic ministries.

It was on the cross that Jesus paid his last tribute of love and honor to his mother. The nails were in his hands and feet and he hung there in agony. He was dying in deepest shame. The obloquy of the world was pouring its blackest tides upon his head. In the throng below, his eye fell on a little group of loving friends, and among them he saw his mother. Full as his heart was of its own anguish, it was not too full to give thought to her.

She would have no protector now. The storms would beat in merciless fury upon her unsheltered head. Besides the bitterness of her bereavement there would be the shame she must endure on his account, the shame of being the mother of one who died on a cross. His heart felt all this and there, in the midst of his own agony, he made provision for her, preparing a home and shelter for her. Amid the dark scenes of the cross his example shines like a star in the bosom of the blackest clouds, saying to us, "Honor thy father and thy mother."

If true honor for parents has its seat in the heart there is little need for rules or detailed suggestions. Yet a few particular ways may be mentioned in which children can add to the happiness and blessedness of the home-life.

They should show their love for their parents by *confiding in them*; not simply by believing in them and trusting their love and their wisdom, but by making them the recipients of all their confidences. A wise parent teaches his child from the very beginning to conceal nothing from him, to tell him everything, and there is no part of the child's life in which he takes no interest. True filial love maintains this openness of heart and life toward a parent, even into the years of maturity. There are no other friends in the world who have so much right to all the confidences of children as their own parents. There are no others in whose breasts the confidences will be so safe; they will never betray the trusts that are placed in them by their own children. There are no others who will take such deep interest in all the events of their daily lives. To the true mother nothing is trifling which has interested her child. She listens as eagerly to the story of its experiences, its joys, its disappointments, its plans, its imaginations, its achievements, as other people listen to the recital of some romantic narrative. She never laughs at its fancies nor ridicules anything that it says or does. Then there are no other friends who are such safe and wise counselors. Some one says that bad advice has wrecked many souls and destinies. The advice of godly and loving parents never wrecks souls. Thousands are wrecked because they will not be guided by it, but none by following it. The children that speak every thought, every hope, every ambition, every plan, every pleasure in the ear of their parents and consult them on every matter, will live safely. At the same time they will confer great happiness upon their parents by confiding so fully in them, for it is a great grief to parents when a child does not confide in them and turns away to others with the sacred confidences of his heart.

Children must learn *self-denial* if they would faithfully do their part. They cannot have everything they desire. They must learn to give up their own wishes for the sake of others. They must learn to do without things that they would like to have. In no other way can home-life be made what it should be. Every member of the family must practice self-denial. The parents make many sacrifices for the children, and it is certainly right that the children early learn to practice self-denial to relieve their parents, to help them and to minister to their comfort.

They should also learn *thoughtfulness*. A home is like a garden of tender plants which are easily broken or bruised. A thoughtless person is for ever causing injury or pain, not through intention, but heedlessly. Many, also, who outside are thoughtful, careful of the feelings of others and quick to speak the gentle word that heals and blesses, at home are thoughtless. But surely there is no place in the world where we ought to be so studiously thoughtful as in our own homes. There are no other friends who love us as do the home friends. There are no other hearts that are so much hurt by our want of thought as are the home hearts.

It does not seem unreasonable to expect, that even

quite young children shall learn to be thoughtful; for those who are older there certainly cannot be a shadow of excuse for rudeness and thoughtlessness. There are in every home abundant opportunities for the culture and display of a thoughtful spirit. Is any one sick? All the others should avoid noise, moving quietly about the house, speaking softly, so as not to disturb the sufferer. All should be gentle to the invalid ministering in every little way brightening the sickroom by their kindness. This thoughtfulness should show itself also toward parents. Oftimes they carry heavy burdens while they go about busying themselves in their daily duties. Their work is hard, or they are in ill health, or they are perplexed and anxious, perhaps on their children's account. Bright, happy, joyous youth never can know what burdens rest heavily on the hearts of those who are older, who are in the midst of life's struggles. It would make us gentle even to strangers to know all their secret griefs; much more would it soften our hearts toward our friends to know what trials they have. If children would remember always that their parents have cares, anxieties and sorrows of which they know not, it would make them gentle at all times toward them. Here is an opportunity for a most helpful ministry, for nothing goes deeper into a parent's heart than the sympathy and gentleness of his own child.

It is not great services that belong to thoughtfulness— only a word of cheer perhaps when one is discouraged a little, tenderness when one looks sad, a little timely help when one is overwrought. It may be nothing more than the bringing of a chair when the father comes in weary, or the running of a little errand for the mother to save her tired fleet, or keeping quiet when the baby is sleeping; or it may be only a gentleness of manner and tone showing warmth within. Thoughtlessness causes no end of pain and care, oftimes of trouble and loss. It goes stalking through heart gardens, treading down the most delicate flowers. It is always saying the wrong word and hurting some one's feelings. It is noisy in the sick-room, rude in the presence of sensitive spirits and cold and unsympathetic toward pain and sorrow. It misses the countless opportunities which intimate daily association with others gives to do really kind deeds, to give joy and help, and instead of such a ministry of blessing it is always causing pain. Its confession must continually be "Ah me!

'The wounds I might have healed,
The human woe and smart!
And yet it never was in my soul
To play so ill a part.
But evil is wrought by want of thought
As well as want of heart.'"

"Oh I did not think," or "I did not mean it," is the poor

excuse most common in many homes. It would be better to learn to think, to think of others, especially of those who love us, and then to walk everywhere, but particularly in our own homes with tender care and regard for the feelings and comfort of others.

Children should early learn to bear some little *share in the home work*. Instead of being always and only a burden to the loving ones who live and toil and sacrifice for them they should seek in every way they can to give help. It was Charles Kingsley who said: "We can become like God only as we become of use." There is a deep truth in his words. We begin to live only when we begin to live to minister to others. Instead of singing "I want to be an angel," it were better if the children should strive to be like the angels, and the angels are ministering spirits sent forth to minister to the heirs of salvation. Home is the school in which we are first to learn and practice the lessons of life. Children should learn there to be useful to their parents and to one another. They can do much in this direction by not requiring unnecessary attendance, by not making trouble and work for others on their account. There are some spoiled children who are such selfish tyrants at home that all the other members of the family are taxed to wait upon them. As soon as possible children should learn to wait upon themselves and in a measure be independent of the help of others, so as to become self-reliant and strong.

What more painful picture do we see than that of sons and daughters growing up idle, too indolent to put forth in their own homes all exertion, too proud to soil their dainty hands with any kind of work, but not too proud to let delicate or already overwrought parents slave to keep them in dainty food or showy array of dress! Nothing good or noble can ever come out of such home-life.

Children should *make themselves worthy of their parents.* They should seek to be all that the father and mother in their most ardent dreams hoped for them. It is a sad thing to disappoint love's brilliant expectations. It matters not so much if mere dreams of earthly greatness fail to come true, for ofttimes the hopes of ambitious parents for their children are only for honors that wither in a day or for wealth that only sinks the soul to ruin. Such hopes were better disappointed. But in the heart of every true Christian parent there glows an ideal of very fair beauty of character and nobleness of soul, which he wants to see his child attain. It is a vision of the most exalted life, lovelier than that which fills the thought of any sculptor as he stands before his marble and begins to hew at the block; fairer than that which rises in the poet's soul as he bows in ecstatic fervor over his page and seeks to describe his dream. Every true, godly parent dreams of the most perfect manhood and womanhood for his children. He wants to see them grow up into Christlikeness, spotless in purity, rich in all the graces, with character fully developed and rounded out in symmetrical beauty, shining in this world, but shining more and more unto the perfect day.

There is a story of a great sculptor weeping like a child as he stood and looked on the fragments of his breathing marble, the work of his life-time and his ripest powers, the dream of his fairest hopes, which lay now shattered at his feet. With still deeper sorrow and bitterer grief do true and godly parents look upon the wreck of their high hopes for their children and the shattering of the fair ideals that glowed in their hearts during the bright years of childhood and youth.

If children would do their part well in return for all the love that has blessed their helpless years and surrounded them in their youth, and that lingers still unwasted in the days of manhood and womanhood they must seek to realize in their own lives all the sacred hopes of their parents' hearts. A wrecked and debauched manhood or a frivolous and purposeless womanhood is a poor return for parental love, fidelity and sacrifice. But a noble life, a character strong, true, earnest and Christlike, brings blessed and satisfying reward to a parent for the most toilsome and painful years of self-forgetting love. Parents live in their children, and children hold in their hands the happiness of their parents. Let them never be untrue to their sacred trust. Let them never bring down the gray hairs of father or mother with sorrow to the grave. Let them be worthy of the love, almost divine, that holds them in its deathless grasp. Let them so live as to be a crown of honor to their parents in their old age. Let them fill their declining years with sweetness and tenderness. Let them make a pillow of peace for their heads when death comes.

When our parents grow old they exchange places, as it were, with us. There were years when we were feeble and helpless, unable to care for ourselves; then they cared for us. They watched over us; they toiled and sacrificed for us; they sheltered us from hardship and trial; they threw around our tender years love's sweetest gentleness and holiest protection. Now we are strong and they are feeble; we are able to endure hardship and toil, but the faintest breath of storm makes them tremble and the lightest toil wearies them. This is the time for us to repay them. It is ours now to show tenderness to them, to shelter them from trial and to pour about them as much of love's tenderness as possible.

> "And canst thou, mother, for a moment think
> That we thy children, when old age shall shed
> Its blanching honors on thy weary head,
> Could from our best of duties, ever shrink?
> Sooner the sun from his high sphere should sink
> Than we, ungrateful, leave thee in that day
> To pine in solitude thy life away,

Or shun thee, tottering on the grave's cold brink.
Banish the thought! Where'er our steps may roam
O'er smiling plains or wastes without a tree,
Still will fond memory point our hearts to thee,
And paint the pleasures of thy peaceful home;
While duty bids us all thy griefs assuage,
And smooth the pillow of thy sinking age."

BROTHERS AND SISTERS

One warm spring day a gentleman tore down an outbuilding that had stood for thirty years. When all the rubbish had been cleared away the spot looked very bare, like a bit of arid desert in the midst of the rich garden that surrounded it. But soon rain fell and then the sun poured down its beams, and in a few days there sprang up countless lovely little flowers, where for thirty years there had been neither life nor beauty, covering the unsightly place and making it one of the fairest spots in all the garden. The seeds must have been lying there in the soil all those years, but, having neither light, moisture nor warmth, they had never grown.

Many a roof covers a home-life that is bare of beauty and joy. Yet all the elements are there that are needed to make it a true image of heaven in its blessedness and peace. In the children growing up together there are the possibilities of a very rich life, with deep joys, fond ties and mutual inspirations. There is wanting only the mighty transforming power of affection to bring out all these possibilities. Surely it is not right that so much blessing should be lost. There is not so much happiness in the world that we can afford to leave our homes desert spots when they might be blossoming gardens. Certainly it is worthwhile to think of the matter, for each of us honestly to inquire whether in our home there are not seeds of beautiful things that are yielding no beauty; whether there are not treasures hidden in our fleeting life which we have never yet discovered; whether we are not blindly passing by Heaven's richest gifts to us of friendship and tender affection lying within our own doors while we press out, quest into other fields and vainly seek for satisfaction.

In every home where there are brothers and sisters there is a field which needs only wise, patient culture to yield life's richest and loveliest things. Are we cultivating this field? Or is it lying neglected, covered, perhaps, with weeds and thorns while we are spending all our strength in trying to make harvests grow on some bare, rocky hillside?

A full and complete family is one in which there are both brothers and sisters, and where all dwell together in tender love. We all know such homes, where the family life is full and the family intercourse close, familiar and happy; where parents and children and brothers and sisters live together in sweet accord, and where the music of the daily life is like an unbroken song of holy peace. Wherever there is such a home its blessedness is almost heavenly.

But it is not thus in every household. There are families

which are complete, so far as numbers go, with both brothers and sisters in the circle, but whose home-life fails to realize the peace and love which I have described. Something is wanting. There may be bitterness and strife or there may be only the absence of all tenderness and of all true and holy fellowship. In either case the story is very sad. A great possible happiness is missed; a great and solemn duty of happiness is neglected and despised. Such a home ought always to be not merely happy, but happy in the deepest, richest, fullest sense. If it fail to be so, great must be the guilt of those who are responsible for the failure. Brothers and sisters have an important duty in the making of the home-life What is their part? Here is a household in which there are two or three sisters, and as many brothers, growing up together. What does each owe to this home? What do they owe the one to the other? How should they live together? What should sisters do for brothers and brothers for sisters? How should sisters help their sisters and brothers help their brothers?

These are a few of the questions which I would like to start in the minds of young people who are living together in the home of their parents. It does not so much matter whether I answer the questions myself or not. If I can merely start them in the minds of those whom they concern, so that they shall go on thinking about them and trying to answer them practically in their lives, this will be far better than the fullest, completest and wisest answers on the pages of this or any book. I shall be quite content therefore if I can merely set up a few emphatic interrogation-points in this chapter.

What should be the home intercourse of brothers and sisters? What should they do toward the home-life? How should they live together? These questions may be answered in general by saying that a close and tender friendship should exist between them. This sounds like a very commonplace remark. Of course brothers and sisters should be friends, and should live together in an intimate relationship as friends. No one denies it. But do we universally find this warm, loving and tender friendship where there are young people in a home? We often find strong ties and attachments, mutual affection and interest, and much that is very beautiful; but when we come closer and look for friendship in the true sense, it is wanting. The brothers and sisters may love one another very truly, but they seek their friends outside the home. They go outside for warm sympathy, for close intimacy, for confidential companionship.

It is not hard to find reasons for this. Living always together and knowing one another from infancy, members of the same family are apt to grow uninteresting to one another. The sameness of the society, day after day, takes away its freshness. The common life which they all lead—

BROTHERS AND SISTERS 149

under the same roof, with the same pursuits, the same
topics for conversation, the same incidents and experience,
the same hopes and fears, the same joys and sorrows, the
same books, the same social life—renders it difficult for the
members of a household to impress one another in
continual repetition and ever kindle inspiration and
emotion the one in the other, as friends from other homes
can do, coming in only now and then.

The fact that it is home and that the ties are natural and
thought to be secure; that the members are sure of each
other, without making any effort to win confidence and
regard; that love between them is a matter of course, as if
by nature, without winning it or cherishing it or troubling
themselves to keep it, is another of the muses for the
absence of real friendship among brothers and sisters. They
imagine that family affection is a sort of instinct not subject
to the laws which control other affections; that it does not
need to be sought or gained or won, as affection must be in
others, by giving affection in return and by the countless
little tendernesses and thoughtfulnesses which are shown to
others whom they desire to win. They forget that the
principle, "he that hath friends must show himself friendly,"
applies in the family just as well as outside of it. They forget
that friendship anywhere must be cherished or it will die;
that indifference and coldness will muse it to wither as
drought causes summer flowers to wither. They imagine, in

a word, that the love of the family is so sure and strong that it needs no care, no pains, to keep it safe. So it is that in very many homes brothers and sisters come and go, day after day, and year after year, mingling in all the life of the household, but never really forming close friendships among themselves.

Friendships in the family require care and culture as do other friendships. We must win one another's love inside the home doors just as we win the love of outside friends. We must prove ourselves worthy; we must show ourselves unselfish, self-forgetful, thoughtful, kind, tender, patient, helpful. Then when we have won each other we must keep the treasure of affection and confidence, just as we do in the case of friends not in the sacred circle of home.

If we have a friend whom we respect and prize very highly, we all know at what pains we are to retain his friendship. We are not sure of it regardless of our treatment of him. We are most careful never to do anything to make us seem unworthy of the friendship. We try to prime from our own character anything that would displease our friend. We cultivate assiduously those qualities of heart and life which he admires. We watch for opportunities to do kindnesses and show favors to him. We guard against whatever would wound or cause him pain. We give him our confidence, we trust him and prove our affection for him in countless ways.

Let no one suppose that home friendships can be won and kept in any other way. We cannot depend on nature or instinct to do this for us. We must live for each other. We must gain each other's heart by giving just what we expect to receive. We must cherish the friendship that we have won. Unless we do, it will not grow. We must watch our words and our conduct. We must seek to please and take pains never to wound or grieve. We must deny self and live for one another. We must confide in one another. We must cultivate in our own hearts and lives whatever is beautiful, whatever is tender, whatever is holy, whatever is true. Friendships in our own home, to be deep and true and heart-satisfying, must be formed by the patient knitting of soul to soul and the growing of life into life, just as in other friendships.

Is it thus in most of our homes? There are distinguished exceptions: there are homes which shine like bits of heaven dropped down upon this sin cursed earth. In these, natural affection has grown into a holy web of real and sacred friendship, binding brothers and sisters in closest bonds. There are brothers who have no friends so close as their own sisters; there are sisters who confide and trust in their own brothers as in no other friends.

One of the tenderest as well as saddest stories of all literature is that of Charles and Mary Lamb. In a fit of insanity the sister had taken the life of her own mother. All her life after this she was subject to periods of frenzy, when it was necessary for her to be confined in an asylum. Then it was that her brother's affection showed itself. He lived for his sister in unselfish devotion. When she was in her right mind she lived with him, and he watched over her with a care that was most touching.

When the fit of insanity was coming on there were premonitory symptoms; they would then start off together for the asylum where for a time she must be confined. One of their friends relates how on one occasion he met the brother and sister weeping bitterly as hand in hand they slowly paced together a little foot-path across the fields, and joining them he found that they were making their solemn way to the accustomed asylum. This was not something that occurred once or twice only, but frequently, and was liable to occur at any time; it was not for a year or two only, but for thirty-five years, until death separated them. He "did not nerve himself to bear his awful charge for a month or for a year; he endured his cross through life, conscious that there was no escape from its burden and from its pains." The indescribable pathos of this story is equaled only by the matchless devotion and constancy of the brother to his sister in all her sad and terrible lot, and by her tender, all-absorbing affection for him. Wordsworth has written of this devoted affection:

"Her love
Was as the love of mothers; and when years,
Lifting the boy to man's estate, had called
The long-protected to assume the part
Of a protector, the first filial tie
Was undissolved; and in or out of sight,
Remained imperishably interwoven
With life itself.

"Through all visitations and all trials
Still they were faithful; like two vessels launched
From the same beach one ocean to explore
With mutual help, and sailing-to their league
True as inexorable winds or bars,
Floating or fixed, of polar ice, allow."

No doubt there are many such deep and real
friendships between brothers and sisters. Between
Wordsworth himself, just quoted, and his sister there was
an attachment which grew with the years and was full of
devotion. In the closing lines of his poem on Tintern Abbey
he pays this tribute to her love and her helpfulness:

"For thou art with me, here upon the banks
Of this fair river; thou my dearest friend,
My dear, dear friend, and in thy voice I catch

The language of my former heart, and read
At former pleasures in the shooting lights
Of thy wild eyes. Oh! yet a little while
May I behold in thee what I was once,
My dear, dear friend."

She lived in and for her brother, and his heart went out in great tenderness toward her. When we read his poems, we read the productions really of two souls in one, for she merged all her interests and gifts in his, "contentedly effacing herself in order that he might become better and higher than he could otherwise have been, and able to render worthier service to the world. The self-sacrifice was complete, but it was crowned by a splendid result."

There is another example of a devoted friendship between brother and sister in the Körners. The brother, Paul Theodor Körner, holds no mean place among German poets. He died at twenty-two, falling in battle. His life was blessed by his sister's devotion, and her affection was nobly returned by him. They lived in mutual confidence. Their friendship was itself "a rare and lovely idyl of grace and beauty." His premature death killed her. She could not bear the shock nor live without him. She survived him only long enough to complete his portrait and to draw with the pencil of love a sketch of his last resting-place. They sleep side by side, so that in death as in life they are not divided. Mrs.

Hemans has commemorated the story of their devotion in these lines:

> "Thou hast a hero's tomb; a lovelier bed
> In hers the gentle girl beside thee lying,
> The gentle girl that bowed her fair young head
> When thou wert gone, in silent sorrow dying.
> Brother, true friend! the tender and the brave—
> "She pined to share thy grave.
>
> "Fame was thy gift from others;—but for her,
> To whom the wide world held that only spot,
> She loved thee! Lovely in your lives ye were,
> And in your early deaths divided not.
> Thou hast thine oaks, thy trophy;—what has she?
> Her own best place—by thee."

The history of life is not all written. Here and there in many a quiet home there is a friendship between brother and sister, on which God's angels look with admiring love, which realizes all that is tender and beautiful in human attachment and affection. Yet I do not think I write a rash word when I say that such friendships are rare. Ofttimes the intercourse of brothers and sisters in the home lacks even the graces of ordinary civility. As soon as the door shuts them within, restraint is thrown off, selfishness comes to the surface, courtesy is laid aside. There is no pleasant conversation. Neither lives for or tries to please the other. The speech is rude or careless and the whole bearing cold or indifferent. The better nature is hidden and the worse comes to the surface. Instead of a tender idyl of grace and beauty, the intercourse of brother and sister is a harsh and painful discord. It should not be so. Brothers and sisters should live together as intimate friends; should carefully win and sedulously keep each other's love, dwelling together in unity and tender affection. There is no friendship in the world so pure, so rich and helpful, as that of the family—if only it be watched and tended as it should be.

Why should not a brother make a confidante of his own sister rather than of any other? Why should not a sister look to her own brother for counsel, for protection, for advice, rather than to any other? Why should not brothers be proud to have their own sisters lean upon their arms? And why should not sisters be proud to look up into the faces of their brothers, and feel secure in the shelter of their manly love? But instead of this what do we often see? The brothers turn away from their own homes to find their companionships and friendships in other circles. As if their own sisters were not worthy of them, or it were a shame for a young man to devote himself in any measure to his sisters, as soon as they are old enough to be their companions they begin to seek other friendships. The sisters are then left to go unprotected or to accept that courtesy and shelter from others which their own brothers have failed to give.

Brothers and sisters are each other's natural keepers. If they fulfilled their duties in this regard, the one to the other, life would show fewer wrecks. They should shield each other. They should be an inspiration to each other in the direction of all noble thought and better life. They should be each other's guardian angels in this world of danger and of false and fatal paths.

Sisters may be their brothers' angels. There is a picture of a child walking on a path that is covered with flowers. Along the edge of the narrow way is shrubbery which hides from the child's sight a deep precipice. The child is unconscious of danger, charmed by the flowers and not seeing how one misstep would hurl it to death. Over the little pilgrim's head hovers a shadowy angel form, scarcely visible, but with eager, loving interest in his eye, while his hand gently touches the child's shoulder; his mission is to guide the child's steps, to shield it from danger and to keep it from falling. The picture represents a truth in the loving providence of God. There are angels who guard, guide, shelter and keep God's children. They are ministering spirits. They keep us in all our ways. Over each one of us a guardian angel hovers unseen evermore. But there is also a most blessed angel ministry of sisters in behalf of their brothers. There is no need to paint here any picture of the perils to which young men are exposed in this world. It makes the heart bleed to see how many of the noblest of them are destroyed, dragged down to ruin, their fair lives blackened, their godlike manhood debauched. They go out of the home pure, with lofty aspirations, with high hope, with brilliant promises, challenging the admiration of all who know them; they come back, how often stained, degraded, hopes wrecked, promises unfulfilled. Every young man who enters life enters a fierce battle in which no truce will come till he either lies down in final defeat or wins the last victory and enters into joy and rest. Life is hard. The young enter it without thought, without anxiety, without serious or solemn sense of danger, because they are not conscious of its true meaning. But, it is one prolonged struggle with enemies and with perils.

> "'What is life, father?'
> 'A battle, my child,
> Where the strongest lance may fail,
> Where the wariest eyes may be beguiled,
> And the stoutest heart may quail;
> Where the foes are gathered on every hand,
> And rest not day or night;
> And the feeble little ones must stand
> In the thickest of the fight.'"

To every young man life is specially hard. As he goes into it he needs the sympathy of all who love him; he needs the prayers and the help of all his friends. For want of the strong support of love many a young man goes down in the battle, and many who come through victorious owe their victories to the holy affection of truly loyal hearts that inspired them with hope and courage in all their hours of struggle. The value of strong friendships never can be known in this world.

Next to mother and father there is no one who can do so much to help a young man to live nobly as his own sister. She cannot always go with him. Her weak arm could not always shield him if she were beside him. But there is a help which she can give him that will prove mightier than her presence. It is not the help of good advice and earnest words—these should have power too—but the help rather of silent and holy influence, gained in the home by a life of unselfishness and beauty, and then held as a potent charm outside and beyond the home walls. There is a power over her brother possible to every true sister, which would be like the very hand of God to guide him and restrain him in all the paths of life. All sisters, however do not have this power over their brothers and, alas! sometimes the power is for evil rather than for good.

May I try to tell you, dear girls, how you can indeed be your brothers' guardian angels? Show them in your own lives at home the perfect grace and beauty of true, noble and lofty womanhood. Strive after all that is delicate, all that is pure, all that is tender, all that is holy and sacred in their divine ideal of woman. Show them in yourselves such perfect loveliness that they will turn away ever after from everything that is unlovely. Make virtue so as they see it embodied in you, that they will always be repelled by vice. Let them see in you such purity of soul, such sweetness of spirit, such divine sanctity, that wherever they go your influence will hang about them like an armor of defense, or, like an angel, hover above their heads in perpetual benediction. Be as nearly a perfect woman, each one of you through Christ's help, as it is possible for you to be. Then when temptations come to your brother there will rise up before his eyes such visions of purity and love that he will turn away with loathing from the tempter.

But oh! if you are not such angels of true womanhood to your brothers, if you do not fill their souls with visions of purity and sweetness, what help do you hope to be to them when they stand in the face of sore temptations? If you are deceitful; if you are selfish; if you are false; if you violate the holy proprieties of modesty and true refinement; if you are frivolous and trifling; if you follow pleasure, turning away from everything serious; if you are careless or heartless, do not deceive yourselves with the vain hope that you can be in any high sense your brothers' guardians in the day of danger. You may advise, you may persuade, you may implore with tears and every token of tender love, when they begin to yield, but your entreaties will avail nothing because your own life has failed to stand the test and to exhibit before them a lofty ideal of womanhood. But if you will only be true, noble, unselfish, gentle, womanly, in the highest, purest sense; if you only are thoughtful and considerate and live for a purpose, making your character decided and strong, you will throw over your brothers silent, imperceptible yet mighty influence, which will be a shield to them in danger, a panoply in temptation, and which will fill their hearts with the purest, loftiest aspirations and aims.

A writer has truthfully said in speaking of a sister's influence upon her brother: "Woman is to him an object of respect or contempt, according to what he sees of his sister's mind and heart. She cannot therefore be too careful in teaching him to respect as well as love her. She cannot confer on him a greater kindness than by giving him an exalted idea of womanhood. She cannot inflict a greater injury than by leading him to think that all women are trifling and heartless, indolent except in the pursuit of pleasure, and greedy of admiration."

> "We know not half the power for good or ill
> Our daily lives possess o'er one another;

A careless word may help a soul to kill,
Or by one look we may redeem our brother.

"'Tis not the great things that we do or say,
But idle words forgot as soon as spoken;
And little thoughtless deeds of every day
Are stumbling-blocks on which the weak are broken."

Brothers should also be their sisters' guardians. Every young man knows what true gallantry is, and what it requires of him. He is to honor every lady, whether rich or poor, whether of higher or lower station, and show her every respect. He is to be to every woman a true knight, ready to defend her from danger, to shield her from every insult, to risk his own life in her behalf. There is no better test of a gentleman than his treatment of women.

Now, to whom ought every young man to show the highest, truest gallantry? To whom ought he first of all to be a most true and loyal knight? To whom if not to his own mother and sisters? Do not they come first in the circle of those to whom he owes honor? Have they not the first claim on his affection? If he is not a true gentleman to his own sisters, can he be at heart a true gentleman to any other woman? Can a young man be manly and treat his own sisters with less respect and honor than he treats other young ladies? Hence a still higher test of a gentleman is his treatment of his own mother and sisters. His chivalry must show itself first toward those who are closest to him in natural ties. He must show them the truest deference. He must treat them with that delicate regard, that gentle, affectionate respect, that tells of the loftiest gallantry. He must consider himself their true knight, whose office it is to throw about them every needed shelter, to serve them, and to promote their highest good in every way.

Of course there is no young man with one spark of the honor of true manliness in his breast who will not instinctively defend his sister, if she is insulted in the street. He will put himself instantly between her and the danger. Neither is there any brother worthy of the name who will not defend the honor of his sister if vile tongues asperse it. But more than this is required of a loyal brother. He should make himself a wall about his sister to shield her from every evil and unholy influence. Every young man knows other young men; he knows their character, their habits, their good and evil qualities. He knows the young men whose lives are impure, who are licentious, who consort with harlots. He knows those who indulge in strong drink, those who are godless and profane, those whose lives are stained with the filth of debauchery. Can he be a true brother and permit such a young man to be the companion of his pure and gentle sister? Can he allow her in the innocence of her heart to accept the attentions of such a young man, to lean upon his arm, to look up into his face with trust? Can he allow her to give her soul's confidences to him? Can he see a friendship forming, strengthening, between his sister and such a young man and remain silent, uttering in her ear no voice of warning or protest, and yet be a loyal and faithful brother to her?

This is a place for plain, strong, and earnest words. Surely young men do not think of this matter seriously or they would require no argument to convince them of their duty. Put the case in the strongest possible form and bring it close to home. You have a sister pure as a lily. She has grown up beside you in the shelter of the home. Her eyes have never looked upon anything vile. Her ears have never heard an impure word. Her soul is white as the snowflakes that fall from the clouds. You love her as you love your own life. You honor her as if she were a queen. A young man seeks to win her regard and confidence. He stands well in society, has good manners, is attractive, intelligent. But you know that he frequents resorts of evil, that his secret life is unchaste, that his soul is stained with low and vile sins, that he is the victim of habits which will bring ruin and dishonor in the end. Your sister knows nothing of his true character. Can you permit him to become her companion? Are you not bound to tell her that he is not worthy of her? Can you do otherwise and be a faithful brother?

Besides this standing between his sister and danger

every brother should also show her in his own life the ideal of the truest, purest, most honorable manhood. If it be true that the best shield a sister can make for her brother is to show him in herself the highest example of womanhood, it is true also that the truest defence a brother can make for his sister is a noble manhood in his own person. He must exhibit before her continually a character without spot or stain, with high aspirations, with generous sympathies, with pure, true, unselfish, Christlike spirit and disposition. If he is going to shield his sister from the impure, he must not be impure himself. He must show her in himself such a high ideal of manhood that her soul shall unconsciously and instinctively shrink from everything that is vulgar, rude or evil. There is no other defence so perfect. Let no brother think that he can be a shelter from evil to his sister if his own life be not unsullied and true.

It must be said also that young ladies should accept, and even seek, the counsel of their brothers with regard to their companions. Let the brothers be true to their sisters, setting before them a lofty example; let them be ready to shield them from danger and to be their wise, faithful counselors; then let sisters look to their brothers for protection and for advice, and be quick to heed the warnings they give and to shun the dangers they point out. Are young women always wise in this regard? Do they desire or receive the counsel of their brothers with regard to companions? Are they always careful enough even when they know young men to be immoral? When a young woman falls into sin the stain always stays upon her name. She can never rise again to her former place. She is excluded from society. She carries the burden of her tarnished name wherever she goes, and though more sinned against than sinning, though the victim of the basest betrayal, she stands thereafter outside the gates, friendless and neglected. Though she repent of her sin and creep to her Saviour's feet and find forgiveness, though the wounded, stricken lamb be laid in the Shepherd's bosom and borne back into his fold; though she be numbered among the children of the Father,—yet society has no forgiveness for her. Her own sister-women have no mercy for her, no place for her by their side, or in their circles.

But what of her betrayer and destroyer? Is he also excluded from society? Is he shunned by the pure who look with so much scorn upon his victim? Is he not still allowed by many young ladies to hold his place, to be honored and welcomed as if there were no stain upon his soul, no crime branding his brow? Are young women true to themselves when they receive to friendship and intimacy one who has proved himself so unworthy of confidence? Let them seek counsel from their own brothers as to the character and fitness of other young men before they receive them to companionship, and accept as friends only such as are worthy of their regard and confidence.

In like manner every young man who has a true sister will do well to take counsel of her concerning other young ladies with whom he would form close friendship. She knows far more than he can possibly know of their real character, and is competent to advise him. He will prove his wisdom by seeking her counsel, especially in forming intimate relationships, which may have so much to do with his whole future.

Indeed, there is no phase of his life into which a young man will not be the better and his life the cleaner and richer for the influence and the help of his sister. Washington Irving wrote these pathetic words concerning the loss he had sustained in his life from having no sisters: "Often have I lamented that Providence denied me the companionship of sisters. Often have I thought that had I been thus favored I should have been a better man. There is many a man who would have been better if he had been blessed with sisters. Every brother who has a sister should cherish her and let his heart go out to her in loyal, manly love. He should prize her love for him as one of the sweetest flowers in earth's garden, one of the most sacred and precious things of life, and he should love her with an affection deep, tender and strong—

"For see, now only see! there's no alloy
Of earth that creeps into the perfect'st gold
Of other loves—no gratitude to claim;
You never gave her life—not even the dross
That keeps life—never tended her, instructed,
Enriched her; so your love can claim no right
O'er hers, save pure love's claim."

Since so much has been said in this chapter of the sister's influence and of the wondrous and subtle charm of her power over her brother, it ought also to be said that not every sister possesses this power. There are many who throw it away. No sister can keep it and be frivolous and trifling. No one can keep it and be a silly butterfly of fashion. To retain it she must be a true, thoughtful, noble woman. She must have a character that shines like crystal in its purity, its sincerity, its simplicity. The power she has and retains must be the power of true womanliness, whose strength is gentleness and whose inspiration is purity of soul.

There is no better place than this to say a few earnest words to young girls on the cultivation of their own hearts. Among all the elements of beauty in the character of a young woman none is more essential than purity of mind and heart, and none gives such grace to the whole life and spirit. Here are a few sentences taken from a private letter:

"True refinement is not mere outside polish. It goes deeper and penetrates to the very foundation of character. It is purity, gentleness and grace in the heart, which, like the perfume of flowers, breathes out and bathes all the life in sweetness. It is not mental culture; there is true refinement often where education has been limited, where in the speech you may detect faults and errors. On the other hand, there is sometimes high intellectual furnishing without any true refinement. That which really refines is purity of mind and heart."

These words are very true. It is not possible even to think of true womanhood without purity. It were as easy to think of a rose without beauty or of a lily without whiteness. Amid the wreck of this world wrought by sin, there are still some fragments of the beauty of Eden and among these none is lovelier than the unsullied delicacy of a true woman's heart. It is possible, too, to preserve this holy purity even amid all this world's sin and foulness. I have seen a lily floating in the black waters of a bog. All about it lay stagnation and vileness, but in the midst of all this the lily remained pure as the robes of an angel. It lay on the dark pond, rocked on the bosom of every ripple, yet never receiving a stain. It held up its unsullied face toward God's blue heaven and poured its fragrance all about it. So is it possible, even in this world of moral evil, for a young woman to grow up, keeping her soul unstained in the midst of it all and ever breathing out the perfume of holy, unselfish love.

On the window of her cell an unhappy girl-queen wrote with a diamond this prayer, "Keep me pure; make others great." This is a fit prayer for every young girl. She should prize nothing in this world so highly as her purity of heart, of thought, of soul. She should be willing to lose anything else—pleasure, wealth, reward—rather than lose this richest jewel. She should guard her imagination, her heart, her affections, that no breath that would sully may ever blow over her life.

There is need here for earnest warning. There are dangers to which every young girl is exposed. There are indications in society of the lowering of the tone of girlhood where there are things in some circles that are painful to every sensitive heart. There are papers and books offered everywhere, and read by too many, which leave a trail of stain on the fair flowers of maidenly refinement. When on a winter's morning you breathe upon the exquisite tracery of frostwork on a window-pane it melts down, and no human hand can ever restore it. Still less is it possible to restore the charm of purity to the soul that has lost it. If a young girl would grow into the most spotless womanhood radiant in every feature with the loveliness of Christ's own image she must from her earliest youth through all the experiences of her life, maintain unsullied purity of heart.

So far the duty only of brothers to sisters and sisters to brothers has been considered. It ought to make a young man's heart exult to have a beautiful and noble sister to lean upon his arm and look up to him for protection, for counsel, for strong, holy friendship. And a sister ought to be proud and happy to have a brother growing into manly strength, to stand by her side, to bear her upon his arm and to shelter her from life's storms. Between brother and sister there should be a friendship deep, strong, close, confiding and faithful.

But the home presents opportunities also for friendships between brother and brother, and between sister and sister. Why should not the brothers of a family stand together there? They have common ties, common joys and sorrows, common interests. The same mother gave them birth and taught their infant lips to lisp the words of prayer. The same father toiled and sacrificed for them. The same home-roof shelters them. Why should they not be to each other the loyalest of friends? When one is in trouble, to whom should his instincts teach him first to turn if not to his own brother? Where should he think to find quicker sympathy and readier help than in his brother's heart and hand? Who should be so willing to give help as a brother!

Yet, do we always find such friendship between brothers? Sometimes we do. There are families of brothers who do stand together in most loyal affection. They share

each other's burdens. If one is in trouble the others gather
close about him with strong sustaining sympathy, as when
one branch of a tree is bruised all the other branches give of
their life to restore the one that is injured. The picture is
very beautiful, and it is what should be seen in every home
in which brothers dwell. But too often it is not seen.
Frequently they drift apart even while they stay under the
home-roof. Each builds up interests of his own. They seek
different friends outside. Sometimes over a father's grave
they quarrel about petty questions of property and unholy
feuds build walls between hearts and lives that should have
been bound together inseparably for ever. With so much in
common with the most sacred ties to bind them together,
and the most holy memories to sanctify their union,
brothers should permit nothing ever to estrange them from
each other. No selfish interest, no question of money or
property, no bitterness or feud should ever come in to sever
their hearts. Though continents divide them and seas roll
between them, their love should remain faithful, strong and
true for ever.

In like manner the sisters in a home should maintain
their friendship for each other through all the changes and
all the varied experiences of life. This they do more
frequently than their brothers. There are many very
beautiful sisterly attachments. Their life within the home
holds them together more closely than brothers are held in

their outside life. They have better opportunities for the cultivation of friendship among themselves in the many hours they sit together at their household work. Then the interests of their lives are less likely to separate them or start differences between them. Nothing is lovelier than the picture of sisters locked in each other's arms, their lives blending in holy love, the one helping the other, giving comfort in sorrow, strength in weakness, and help in trial.

Are the brothers and sisters who read these pages realizing in their own lives the ideals which have here been even so imperfectly sketched? Are they living together in tender love in their own home? If they are, Heaven's benediction will fall upon their hearts and lives like a baptism of holy peace. If they are not, where is the fault? What can be done to correct it? Too many blessed possibilities of joy, of love, and of helpfulness lie in these sacred relationships to be neglected or ruthlessly tossed into the dust. Life is too short to be spent in strife and discord anywhere, especially in the holy circle of the home. Strifes and alienations here are the seeds for a harvest of sorrow. Sad, sad will it be to stand by the coffin of a brother or a sister, and while we look at the cold, silent clay, remember that we were ever unkind to one who stood so near, that we ever failed in acts of love, or that we ever allowed anything to estrange us or make our intercourse cold and formal.

Have you brothers or sisters living anywhere in this great world? Have you allowed the friendship to grow cold or the ties to be forgotten? Have you permitted all intercourse to be broken off? Lose not a day till you have done the first thing, taken the first step, to gather up the shattered links and reunite them in a holy chain. If they are far away, write to them in words of love. If they are within reach, go to them in person. If you are still living side by side in the old home, and if your life together has not been close, intimate, confiding and helpful, seek at once by all the wise arts of a loving heart to make it what it ought to be.

Then, no matter how plain, simple or old-fashioned your home may be, the sacred friendships beneath its roof will transfigure it all. Poverty is a light cross if there is love at home. Toil, hardships, care, sacrifice, and even sorrow lose their ruggedness, bleakness, and severity when tender affection twines over them as cold, bare, rugged rocks are changed into beauty when the wild vines wreath them all over with festoons of green and gentle smiling flowers grow from every crevice and fill every black nook and fissure.

"Dear moss," said the thatch on an old ruin, "I am so worn, so patched, so ragged; really I am quite unsightly. I wish you would come and cheer me up a little; you will hide all my infirmities and defects, and, through your loving sympathy, no finger of contempt or dislike will be pointed at me." "I come," said the moss; and it crept up and around and in and out, until every flaw was hidden and all was smooth and fair. Presently the sun shone out and the old thatch looked bright and fair, a picture of rare beauty in the golden rays. "How beautiful the thatch looks!" cried one who saw it. "How beautiful the thatch looks!" said another. "Ah!" said the old thatch, "rather let them say, 'How beautiful is the loving moss that spends itself in covering up all my faults, keeping the knowledge of them all to herself, and by her own grace making my age and poverty wear the garb of youth and luxuriance!'"

Is your home plain and bare? Must you meet hardships and endure toil? Have you cares and privations? Do you sigh for something finer, more beautiful, less hard? Call up love to wreathe itself over all your home-life. Cultivate home friendships. Bind up the broken home ties. Plant the flowers of affection in every corner. Then soon all will be transfigured. You will forget care, hardships and toil, for they will all be hidden under lovely garments of affection. Your eye will see no more the homeliness, the hardness, the anxieties, the toils, but will be charmed with the luxuriance of love that shall cover every blemish.

THE HOME-LIFE

In a quiet nook among the hills, where great forest trees interlock their branches and form a deep shade, a little stream takes its rise. It springs out from among the rocks and goes rippling over the stones, only a tiny thread of silver at first as it begins its way toward the great sea. Other streamlets join it as it flows, and it goes on gathering and increasing in volume, until it becomes a river, bearing commerce on its bosom, and emptying at last into the broad ocean.

Its course is marked by great variety. For a time it goes laughing and dancing over the stones, like a child at play, with merriment and glee. As it grows wider and deeper it becomes soberer and graver and its motion is slower; and when it is a river its flow is calm and majestic. Sometimes its course lies in the sunshine, its waters sparkling like crystal in the bright rays; sometimes it runs through meadows and fields where sweet flowers bloom on its banks; sometimes it plunges into deep, dark gorges, between high rocks, where no sunbeam ever falls and no flower ever blooms; sometimes it breaks into a mad swirl or rushes away in a fierce torrent or leaps over a precipice in a foaming cataract. So it flows on, amid all this diversity of scene and experience, until it reaches the wide sea.

Is not all this a picture of the life of every true home? It begins when two young lives meet and blend in one, and at the marriage altar with clasped hands vow to love and cherish each the other until death shall separate them. It starts amid flowers and pealing bells and sweet strains of music and congratulations of friends. In its earliest course it is like the singing brook as it ripples away in its pebbly channel, without care or serious thought, merry and gladsome, bright and sparkling, but without great depth or meaning. In some sense these are happy days, yet their happiness is superficial and does not take deep hold on life.

A little later and the current begins to deepen and widen. Other lives enter the stream of the home-life as one by one the children come. After that there may be less glee and merriment, just as the stream grows calmer and quieter with its increasing volume. There is more care. Anxieties creep into the life. Thoughtlessness gives way to seriousness as responsibilities are added. New burdens accumulate. Life takes on a deeper meaning. There is less of laughing lightheartedness perhaps, but the joy is deeper and more real.

As the years pass on, the experiences of the home-life are diversified by many a change and vicissitude, by many an alternation of joy and sorrow. There are times of kindness and prosperity, as when the stream flows through quiet valleys, and green slopes stretch away from its banks and sweet flowers kiss its silvery waters. Then there are times of sorrow, when the peaceful current is broken, when the stream plunges into the gloomy chasm. Every home has its experiences of trial. But through these it passes, emerging again, and flowing on, calmer, deeper, more majestic, in richer, fuller life than before, until at last it enters the great sea of eternity.

In the foregoing chapters the part of each member of the family in the making of the home has been considered. The duties and responsibilities of the husband, of the wife, of the parents, of the children, of brothers and of sisters, have been touched upon. If all the different members of a family are faithful in their own places, doing their own part well, the home-life will be a sweet song of holy peace. Whatever its experiences may be, it will always have its undertone of joy. Its lamps of affection no wintry blast can put out. Secluded from the world, sheltered by its own roof, containing in itself the sources of happiness and not dependent upon the outside world for its gladness and joy, it matters little whether it be day or night, whether it be calm or stormy, without. The true home has a peace that is not broken by earth's tempests. Its love is a fountain of blessing that does not waste in summer weather, and its happiness and blessing in household life are simply incalculable. All that is needed is that each member faithfully do his own part.

It may be profitable at this point to touch upon a few of the particular phases and incidents of home-life common to all households. There is nothing insignificant in the life that we live within our own doors. There is nothing that is without influence in the building up of character.

There is something infinitely more important than the mere recent performance of duties. There is an unconscious influence that hangs about every life like an atmosphere, which is more important than the words or acts of the life. There are many parents who fail in no duty, who are deeply anxious for their children, who really strive to make their home what it should be, and whose influence is not a benediction. When the results of life are all gathered up it will probably be seen that the things which have made the deepest and most lasting impressions in our homes and upon our children have not been the things we did with purpose and intention, planning to produce a certain effect, but the things we did when we were not thinking of training or influencing or affecting any other life. A wise writer says, "I look with wonder on that old time, and ask myself how it is that most of the things I suppose my father and mother built on especially to mould me to a right manhood are forgotten and lost out of my life.

But the things they hardly ever thought of—the shadow of blessing cast by the home, the tender, unspoken love, the sacrifices made and never thought of, it was so natural to make them, ten thousand little things so simple as to attract no notice and yet so sublime as I look back at them,—they fill my heart still and always with tenderness when I remember them and my eyes with tears."

It is not so much strict fidelity in teaching and training that is powerful in our homes for holy impression as it is the home-life itself. The former is like the skillful trimming and training of a vine; the latter is like the sunshine and the rain that fall upon the vine. The writer above quoted adds: "It is said that a child, hearing once of heaven, and that his father would be there, replied, 'Oh! then I dinna want to gang.' He did but express the instinct of a child to whom the father may be all that is good, except just goodness; and be all that any child can want, except what is indispensable—that gracious atmosphere of blessing in the healing shadow it exists without which even heaven would come to be intolerable."

It is necessary that the whole home-life and home-spirit should be in harmony with the teaching and training, if these are to make holy impressions. Simple goodness is more important than the finest theories of home government most thoroughly and faithfully carried out. There is nothing in the daily routine of the family life that is unimportant. Indeed, it is ofttimes the things we think of as without influence that will be found to have made the deepest impression on the tender lives of the household.

A distinguished Danish artist had chiseled in the city of Rome some of his rarest works in marble. When he had finished them they were sent home. The workmen, as they unpacked them carelessly, scattered on the ground the straw which had been wrapped about the statues. In the straw were multitudes of little seeds, and the next summer countless flowers from the gardens of Rome were blooming all about the artist's northern home. He had not intended to drop these tiny seeds of loveliness; he was intent only on his great work, thinking only of the magnificent results in marble that he was bringing home which would be admired for ages. But while carrying out his grand purposes he was also unconsciously scattering about his home other tender and beautiful influences. In like manner the busiest men, intent on the grandest purposes, are ever scattering about them countless seeds which will spring up either in tender loveliness to bless their homes or in a harvest of evil to leave blight and sorrow. It may be that, in the end, the unconscious, unintended influences will far surpass in their permanent results of life and character those for which they planned with such pains and wrought with such glowing hope.

Few things are more important in a home than its

conversation, and yet there are few things to which less thought is given. The power of communication, which lies in the tongue, is simply incalculable. It can impart knowledge; utter words that will shine like lamps in darkened hearts; speak kindly sentences that will comfort sorrow or cheer despondency, breathe out thoughts that will arouse and quicken heedless souls; even whisper the secret of life-giving energy to spirits that are dead.

"Only a word, but 'twas spoken in love,
With a whispered prayer to the Lord above;
And the angels in heaven rejoice once more,
For a new-born soul entered in by the door."

The good we could do in our homes with our tongues if we would use them to the utmost limit of their capacity is simply impossible to compute. Why should so much power for blessing be wasted? Especially why should we ever pervert these gifts and use our tongues to do evil, to give pain, to scatter seeds of bitterness? It is a sad thing when a child is born dumb, but it were better far to be dumb and never to have the gift of speech at all, than, having it, to employ it in speaking only sharp, unloving or angry words.

"Only a word!
But sharp, oh sharper than a two-edged sword,

To pierce and sting and sear

The heart whose peace a breath of flame could war."

The home conversation should be loving. Home is the place for warmth and tenderness. Yet there is in many families a great dearth of kind words. In some cases there is no conversation at all worthy of the name. There are no affectionate greetings in the morning or good—nights at parting when the day closes. The meals are eaten in silence. There are no fireside chats over the events and incidents of the day. A stranger might mistake the home for a deaf and dumb institution. In other cases it were better if silence reigned, for only words of miserable strife and shameful quarreling are heard from day to day. Husband and wife, who vowed at the marriage altar to cherish one the other till death, keep up an incessant petty strife of words. Parents who are commanded in the holy word not to provoke their children to anger lest they be discouraged, but to bring them up in the nurture of the Lord, scarcely ever speak gently to them. They seem to imagine that they are not "governing" their children unless they are perpetually scolding at them. They fly into passions against them at the smallest irritation. They issue their commands to them in words and tones which would better suit the despot of some petty savage tribe than the head of a Christian household. It is not strange that under such "nurture" the children, instead of dwelling together in unity, with loving speech, should only wrangle and quarrel, speaking only bitter words in their intercourse with one another. That there are many homes of just this type it is idle to deny. That prayer is offered morning and evening in these families only makes the matter worse, as it is mockery for a household to rise from their knees only to begin another day of strife and bitterness.

Nothing in the home-life needs to be more carefully watched and more diligently cultivated than the conversation. It should be imbued with the spirit of love. No bitter word should ever be spoken. The language of husband and wife in their intercourse together should always be tender. Anger in word, or even in tone, should never be suffered. Chiding and faultfinding should never be permitted to mar the sacredness of their speech. The warmth and tenderness of their hearts should flow out in every word that they utter to each other. As parents, too, in their intercourse with their children, they should never speak save in words of Christlike gentleness. It is a fatal mistake to suppose that children's lives can grow up into beauty in an atmosphere of strife. Harsh, angry words are to their sensitive souls what frosts are to the flowers. To bring them up in the nurture of the Lord is to bring them up as Christ himself would, and surely that would be with infinite gentleness. The blessed influence of loving speech day after day and month after month is impossible to estimate. It is like the falling of warm spring sunshine and rain on the garden, causing lovely flowers to spring up in every nook and corner, and filling all the air with sweet fragrance. Only beauty and gentleness of character can come from such a home.

> "I have known a word more gentle
> Than the breath of summer air;
> In a listening heart it nestled,
> And it lived for ever there.
> Not the beating of its prison
> Stopped it ever, night or day;
> Only with the heart's last throbbing
> Could it fade away."

But home conversation needs more than love to give it its full influence. It ought to be enriched by thought. The Saviour's warning against idle words should be remembered. Every wise-hearted parent will seek to train his household to converse on subjects that will yield instruction or tend toward refinement. The table affords an excellent opportunity for this kind of education. Three times each day the family gathers there. It is a place for cheerfulness. Simply on hygiene grounds meals should not be eaten in silence. Bright, cheerful conversation is an excellent sauce and a prime aid to digestion. If it prolongs the meal, and thus appears to take too much time out of the busy day, it will add to the years in the end by increased healthfulness and lengthened life. In any case, however, something is due to refinement, and still more is due to the culture of one's home-life. The table should be made the centre of the social life of the household. There, all should appear at their best. Gloom should be banished. The conversation should be bright and sparkling. It should consist of something besides dull and threadbare commonplaces. The weather is a worn-out topic. The idle gossip of the street is scarcely a worthy theme for such hallowed moment.

The conversation of the table should be of a kind to interest all the members of the family; hence it should vary to suit the age and intelligence of those who form the circle. The events and occurrences of each day may with profit be spoken of and discussed, and now that the daily newspaper contains so full and faithful a summary of the world's doings and happenings, this is easy. Each one may mention the event which has specially impressed him in reading. Bits of humor should always be welcome, and all wearisome recital and dull, uninteresting discussion should be avoided.

Table-talk may be enriched, and at the same time the intelligence of all the members of a family may be advanced, by bringing out at least one new fact at each meal, to be added to the common fund of knowledge. Suppose there are two or three children at the table ranging in their ages from five to twelve. Let the father or the mother have some particular subject to introduce during the meal which will be both interesting and profitable to the younger members of the family. It may be some historical incident, or some scientific fact, or the life of some distinguished man. The subject should not be above the capacity of the younger people for whose especial benefit it is introduced, nor should the conversation be overladen by attempting too much at one time. One single fact clearly presented and firmly impressed is better than whole chapters of information poured out in a confused jargon on minds that cannot remember any part of it. A little thought will show the rich outcome of a system like this if faithfully followed through a series of years. If but one fact is presented at every meal there will be a thousand things taught to the children in a year. If subjects are wisely chosen the fund of knowledge communicated this way will be of no inconsiderable value. A whole system of education lies in this suggestion, for besides the communication of important knowledge, the habit of mental activity is stimulated, interest is awakened in lines of study and research which afterward may be followed out, tastes are improved, whilst the whole effect upon the family life is elevating and refilling.

It may be objected that such a system of table-talk could not be conducted without much thought and preparation on the part of parents. But if the habit once were formed and the plan properly introduced it would be found comparatively easy for parents of ordinary intelligence to maintain it. Books are now prepared in great numbers giving important facts in small compass. Then there are encyclopaedias and dictionaries of various kinds. The newspapers contain every week paragraphs and articles of great value in such a course. A wise use of scissors and paste will keep scrapbooks well filled with materials which can readily be made available. It will be necessary to think and plan for such a system, to choose the topics in advance, and to become familiar with the facts. This work might be shared by both parents, and thus be easy for both. That it will cost time and thought and labor ought not to be an objection, for is it not worth almost any cost to secure the benefits and advantages which would result from such a system of home instruction?

These are hints only of the almost infinite possibilities of good which lie in the home conversation. That so little is realized in most cases where so much is possible is one of the saddest things about our current life. It may be that these suggestions, though crude, may stimulate in some families at least an earnest search after something better than they have yet found in their desultory and aimless conversational habits. Surely there should be no home in which, amid all the light talk that flies from busy tongues, time is not found every day to say at least one word that shall be instructive, suggestive, elevating or in some way helpful.

The home evenings present another field rich with possibilities of lasting influence and holy impression. It is one of the misfortunes of our times that the home is being so robbed of its evenings by business, by pleasure, and by society. Some men never spend an evening at home in all the year. Some women do little better. Is it any wonder that in such cases Heaven's benediction does not seem to fall upon the household? The days are so full of occupation for most of us, from early morning till nightfall, that whatever real home-life we make we must make in the evenings. "To the evening, and especially the winter's evening, belong mainly the influences of domestic life. Its few short hours are all the uninterrupted time we have at our disposal to know our own or be known of them. The impression that home leaves upon the child comes largely from its evenings. The visions which memory delights in conjuring up are the old scenes about the evening fire or the evening lamp."

When we think of the importance of the evenings at home it certainly seems worthwhile to plan to save as many as possible of them from outside demands for the sacred work within. It were better that we should neglect some social attraction, or miss some political meeting, or be absent from some lodge or society, than that we should neglect the culture of our own homes and let our children slip away from us for ever. To allow a boy to spend his evenings on the streets is almost inevitably to indenture him to a life of sin, ending in ruin. The school of the street trains him with amazing rapidity for all manner of crimes. The father who permits his son to go out nightly from the home door amid these unholy influences must not be surprised to learn in a very little time that his boy has learned to smoke, to swear, to drink, to gamble, and that his soul has already been debauched.

But how can we keep our boys off the streets at nights? Can we do it if we ourselves hasten away from home every evening as soon as we snatch a harried supper? If parents would save their boys they must make a home-life for the evenings so pleasant, so attractive, so charming that they will not want to leave it for any coarse or glaring fascinations outside. How can this be done? It can be done if the parents set themselves to do it. There may be a season of romping if the children are young—a children's hour devoted to such play as they will enjoy. There may be pleasant games to pass away a portion of the evening. There may be the reading aloud of some interesting book by one member of the family while the others carry on the light forms of work which occupy their hands and eyes but leave their ears open to hear. There may be music for a time and bright, cheerful conversation, closing with a prayer and a goodnight.

No instruction is needed to teach any intelligent parent how to give to the evenings at home a charm which shall make their influence all-potent. It is necessary only that parents shall set about doing that which their own hearts tell them so plainly ought to be done. Of course it will take time. Something must be left out of life if this is to be done. But is there anything else in all the round of life's calls, and even its seeming duties, that might not well be left out for the sake of anchoring our children to their homes? Is there anything else that it would be so fatal and terrible to leave out as to leave our children out to perish in the ruin of the streets, while we are at lodges and operas and parties, or even at church meetings?

In considering the influences in the home-life that leave deep and permanent impressions on character, thought must be given to the books and papers that are read. The invention of the art of printing marked a new era in the world's history. On the printed pages that fly everywhere like the leaves of autumn, drifting to our doors and swept into our innermost chambers, are borne to us the golden thoughts of the best and wisest men and women of all ages. The blessings that the print scatters are infinite and rich beyond all estimate. But the same types that to-day give us pure and holy thoughts, words of truth and of life, to-morrow give us veiled suggestions of evil, words of honeyed sweetness, but in which deadly poison is concealed. It is related that one of the soldiers of Cyrus found a casket which was reported to be full of valuable treasures. It was opened, and out of it came a poisonous atmosphere which caused a terrible plague in the army. Many a book that is bound in bright colors has stored within those covers the most deadly moral influences. To open it in a pure home, among young and tender lives, is to let loose evils that never can be gathered back and locked up again.

The printing-press puts into the hands of parents a means of good which they may use to the greatest advantage in the culture of their home-life and in the shaping of the lives of their household. But they must keep a most diligent watch over the pages that they introduce. They should know the character of every book and paper that comes within their doors, and should resolutely exclude everything that would defile. Then, while they exclude everything whose influence would be for evil, if they are wise they will bring into their home as much as possible of pure, elevating, and refining literature. Every beautiful thought that enters a child's mind adds to the strength and loveliness of the character in after days. The educating influence of the best books and papers is incalculable, and no parent can afford to lose it in the training of his family.

Something should be said about home pleasures and amusements. It is a great misfortune if parents suffer themselves to lose the youthful spring and elasticity out of their lives, and to grow away from the spirit of childhood. They should never become old in heart. It was Swedenborg who wrote of heaven that there the oldest angels are the youngest. There is something very striking in the thought. In that blessed Home the members of the family grow always toward youth. Instead of acquiring the marks of age, of care, of exhaustion, they become every day fresher, fairer, fuller of the exuberance of life. It ought to be so in every true earthly home. We cannot stop the years from rolling on, nor can we keep back the gray hairs and the wrinkles and the lines of weariness. These bodies will grow old in spite of us. But there is no reason why our spirits should not be always young. We ought to keep a child's heart beating in our breast until God calls us up higher. We ought to grow always toward youth. The oldest people in the home ought to be the youngest. If we do grow old it will be bad for our households. There are some homes where the children can scarcely smile without being frowned upon. They are expected to be as grave as if they were fifty and carrying all the burdens of the world upon their shoulders. All the joyousness of their nature is repressed. They are taught to be prim and stiff in their manners. They are continually impressed with the thought that it is a sinful time to play and that it is displeasing to God to have fun and frolic. Some one says, "A great many homes are like the frame of a harp that stands without strings. In form and outline they suggest music, but no melody rises from the empty spaces; and thus it happens that home is unattractive, dreary and dull." There are homes which this picture describes, but they are not the homes that are most like heaven, nor the homes out of which come the truest and noblest lives.

God wants us to fill our homes with happiness. He made childhood joyous, full of life, bubbling over with laughter, playful, bright and sunny. It is a crime to repress the mirth and the gladness and to try to make children grave and stately. Life's burdens will come soon enough to lie upon their shoulders. Life will soon enough bring care and anxiety and hardship and a weight of responsibility. We should let them be young and free from care just as long as possible. We should put into their childhood days just as much sunshine and gladness, just as much cheerful pleasure as possible. Besides the way also to make them strong and noble in character when they grow up to manhood and womanhood is to make their childhood and youth both bright and happy. If you want to produce a vigorous, healthy plant, you will not bring it up in a dark room; you will give it all the sunshine it will take. Human lives will never grow into their best in gloom. Pour the sunshine about them in youth; let them be happy; encourage all innocent joy; provide pleasant games for them; romp and play with them; be a child again among them. Then God's blessing will come upon your home, and your children will grow up sunny-hearted, gentle, affectionate, joyous themselves and joy-bearers to the world.

When MacMahon returned victorious from the battle of Magenta, all Paris came out to welcome him. Many were the honors heaped upon the brave, bronzed soldier. As he was passing in triumph through the streets and boulevards, a little child ran out toward him with a bunch of flowers in her hand. He stooped down and lifted her up before him, and she stood there, her arms twining about his neck, as he rode on. This simple exhibition of gentleness toward a little child pleased the people more, and seemed a more beautiful act in their eyes for the moment than all the memory of his heroic deeds on the battlefield. Men are greatest and best, not when they are wrestling with the world, not when they are putting forth the startling qualities of power, not when they are playing the hero in great contests, but when they are exhibiting most of the spirit of a little child. No parent therefore should ever be ashamed to romp and play with his children. Perhaps he is nearer to God then than when doing what he deems his grandest work in the world. Perhaps the angels applaud more then than when he is performing deeds that bring him praise or fame; and it is better to have fame among the angels than in a dozen worlds.

The young must have amusements. The only question is, What shall be the character of the amusements? Shall they be pure, healthful, refining, elevating? Or shall they be degrading in their influence? The parents must answer these questions, and the best way to answer them is to provide in their own home such amusements as they deem proper. If the home is dull and cheerless it must not be considered an indication of extraordinary depravity that the children and young people seek pleasure elsewhere. It is as natural that bees hived in a stubble-field should want to fly over the fence to gather honey from the clover-field adjoining. If there is clover at home they will not care to fly abroad. Wise parents will provide amusements for their children, and they will provide them at home, and thus count the solicitations of worldly pleasure outside.

There is a great variety of suitable home amusements. One is music. Music is not a mere amusement only, but one that combines rich instruction and lasting influence for good with the purest enjoyment. It is scarcely possible to conceive of any pleasure that surpasses an evening of song in the parlor when the whole family unites in it, perhaps with other friends, one at the piano or organ and the others grouped about, male and female voices blending, now in the pleasant ballad or glee, now in the sacred anthem or hymn. The songs of childhood sung thus into the heart are never forgotten. Their memories live under all the accumulations of busy years, like the sweet flowers that bloom all the winter beneath the heavy snowdrifts. They are remembered in old age when nearly all else is forgotten, and ofttimes sing themselves over again in the heart with voice sweet as an angel's when no other music has power to charm. They neglect one of the richest sources of pleasure and blessing who do not cultivate singing in their homes.

Then there are many games which bring great enjoyment. Chess is delightful to those who have patience and skill to master it, but it requires close thought. There is much enjoyment in the old-fashioned game of checkers. There are many games with various kinds of historical cards, and cards of authors or of birds and animals, which combine exciting pleasure with some instruction. There is scarcely any limit to the number of innocent games from which to make selection for evening amusements. Charades furnish genuine enjoyment. Reading clubs may be so conducted as to yield both pleasure and instruction.

It needs only a heart in full sympathy with youthful feelings, a little skill in arranging and preparing these pleasures, small expense in furnishing the simple games and other requisites, and interest enough in the matter to devote a little time and pains to it. There is no parent of ordinary intelligence who may not make his home-life so bright and sunny that no one will ever care to go outside to seek amusement amid the senseless frivolities or the debasing pleasures that the world offers. Homes that are made thus in all these ways so bright and happy acquire a resistless power over those who live within their doors, which will hold them under its subtle influence wherever they go in all their after years.

There is one experience that comes sooner or later in the life of every home—the experience of sorrow. There may be years of unbroken gladness, but in the end grief is sure to come. The stream that has flowed so long with merry ripple through the green fields and amid the flowers in the bright sunshine, sweeps into the deep shadows, plunges into the dark, sunless gorge, or is hurled over the waterfall. We press our children to our bosom today, and love builds up a thousand brilliant hopes for them in our hearts; then tomorrow death comes and they lie silent and still amid the flowers. Or we watch over them and see them grow into nobleness and beauty when just as our dreams and hopes seem about to be realized, the fatal touch is upon them and they are taken away.

There is no need to describe this experience, memory needs no reminder in such cases. The most helpful thing that can be done in these pages is to point out a few of the comforts which should come to every Christian home in such hours. There is great comfort in the thought that what has befallen us is God's will. Long ago this was the rock on

which a godly man leaned when death had come suddenly
and taken all: "The Lord gave, and the Lord hath taken
away." When we know that God is truly our Father and that
his love is eternal and unchangeable, this confidence should
give us great peace even in the sorest bereavement. In the
Pitti Palace at Florence there are two pictures which hang
side by side. One represents a stormy sea with its wild waves
and black clouds and fierce lightning flashing across the sky.
In the waters a human face is seen, wearing an expression of
the utmost agony and despair. The second picture also
represents a sea tossed by as fierce a storm, with as dark
clouds; but out of the midst of the waves a rock rises, against
which the waters dash in vain. In a cleft of the rock are some
tufts of grass and green herbage, with sweet flowers, and
amid these a dove is seen sitting on her nest quiet and
undisturbed by the wild fury of the storm or the mad
dashing of the waves about her. The first picture fitly
represents the sorrow of the world, where all is helpless
despair, and the other the sorrow of the Christian where
amid trial just as terrible, he is in perfect peace, because he
is hidden in the cleft of the Rock of Ages and nestles
securely in the arms of God's unchanging love.

Another of the great comforts when a little child is
taken away is the truth of the immortal life. In the autumn
days the birds leave our chill northern clime and we hear
their songs no more; but the birds are not dead. In the

warmer clime of the far South they live, and amid flowers and fragrant foliage and luscious fruits they continue to sing as joyously as they sang with us in the happiest summer day. So our children leave us, and we miss their sweet faces and prattling voices; but they have only gone to the summer-land of heaven. There in the midst of the glory of the Lord they dwell, shedding their tender grace on other hearts. We all believe this, but most of us believe it in such a way as to get but little comfort from it. The bringing into our hearts of the truth of immortality would take away all bitterness from our sorrow when our little ones leave us.

One of the chief elements of the sorrow when children or young persons die is the sore disappointment. Careers of great usefulness have been marked out for them, and without even entering upon them they are gone. They seem to have lived in vain, to have died without accomplishing any work in this world. So, it appears until we think more deeply of it, then we see that they have not been in this world in vain, though their stay was so brief. They have not done what we had planned for them to do, but they have accomplished the part in God's great Plan which he had marked out for them.

Here is a little babe; it lies now in the coffin with a face beautiful as an angel's smile. It lived but a few days or a few months. It merely opened its eyes upon the earth and then, as if too pure for this world of sin, closed them again and went back to God. Did you say that it lived in vain, that it performed no work? Do you know how many blessings it brought down from heaven to that home when it came like a messenger from the fragrant garden of God, shook its robes and then fled away again? It only crept into the mother's bosom for a brief season and was gone, but ever afterward her heart will be warmer, her life richer and deeper, and her spirit gentler and sweeter. No one can tell what holy work a babe performs that stays only an hour in this world. It does not live in vain. It leaves touches of beauty on other souls which never shall fade out. It may accomplish more in that one short hour, leave greater blessings behind, than do others who live long full years. It may change the eternal destiny of one or more souls. Many a child dying leads an unsaved parent to the sacred feet of Christ. Certain it is that no true parent is ever just the same in character after clasping his own child in his arms. To have felt the warmth and thrill of a new love even for a few moments, though the object loved be withdrawn, leaves a permanent result in the life.

Or perhaps the child lives to be ten or twelve years old. She is the light and joy of the home. Great promises begin to bud and blossom within her life. Then she dies. As the parents bend over her and kiss her pale, cold lips, they mourn over the crushed hopes that lie there, like buds opening only to be killed by the frost. In imagination they have seen her standing forth in all the splendor of queenly womanhood crowned with honor, beauty, and love. But she has died without realizing these. She has fallen just on the threshold of life. Yet who will say that she did no work in those brief, bright years? She has been a blessing in her home all the time, drawing out the love of tender hearts, scattering influences of joy and purity. Now she is gone, but the work she has done in the home, hearts, and lives remains and never can be taken away.

God takes away your children, and in faith you surrender them to him to see them no more in this world; but you cannot give back all that they have brought to you. In your heart new springs of love were opened by their coming; and you cannot give these back. Death cannot take out of your life the new experiences which you had in pressing them to your heart or in loving and caring for them through the sunny years. You are better, stronger, richer in your nature, more a man or a woman, because you have held in your arms and have nurtured your own child. These new outreachings of your life never can be taken from you. Like new branches of a tree they will remain ever after part of yourself. Though the loved ones are removed, the results of their coming to you and staying with you, the influences, the impressions made, the qualities, the new growths in your life will never depart. They are your permanent possessions forever. Tennyson puts this truth in happy phrase:

> "God gives us love; something to love
> He lends us; but when love is grown
> To ripeness, that on which it throve
> Falls off; and love is left alone."

Thus when the influences of a child's life remain, its death also brings new blessings to the home. It softens all hearts. Rudeness grows gentle under the influence of sorrow. It brings the parents closer together. Many an incipient estrangement is healed at the coffin of a dead child. It is like a new marriage.

> "I thought our love at full, but I did err;
> Joy's wreath drooped o'er mine eyes; I could not see
> That sorrow in our world must be
> Love's deepest spokesman and interpreter."

> "I felt instantly
> Deep in my soul another bond to thee
> Thrill with that life we saw depart from her.
> O mother of our angel child I twice dear!
> Death knits as well as parts, and still, I wish,
> Her tender radiance shall enfold us here,
> Even as the light, borne up by inward bliss,

Threads the void grooms of space without a fear,
To print on farthest stars her pitying kiss."

* James Russell Lowell.

There come to many homes other sorrows besides the
sorrows of bereavement. There are griefs sorer than those
caused by death. There are sorrows over the living who are
in peril or who are wandering away, sometimes over those
who have fallen. There are wives weeping in secret over
trials of which they can speak to none but God. There are
parents with sadder disappointments than if they stood by
the coffins of their early dead. Sin and shame cause bitterer
tears than death. There are homes from which the shadow
never lifts, out of which the brightness seems for ever to
have gone. There are home hearts from which the music
has fled, and which are like harps with their strings all
broken. Yet even for these there is comfort if they are
resting in God's bosom. The divine love can bring blessing
out of every possible trial. No life that clings by faith to
Christ can be destroyed.

In a lovely Swiss valley there is a cascade which is
caught by the swift winds as it pours over the edge of the
rock, and scattered so that the falling stream is lost for the
time, and only a wreath of whirling spray is seen in the air.
But farther down the valley the stream gathers itself back

again and pours along in full current in quiet peace, as if it had never been so rudely smitten by the wind. Even the blast that scatters it for the time, and seems to destroy it altogether, really makes it all the lovelier as it whirls its crystal drops into the air. At no other point in all its course is the Staubbach so beautiful. There are Christian lives that seem to be utterly destroyed by trial, but beyond the sorrow they move on again in calmer, fuller strength, not destroyed, not a particle of their real life wasted. And in the trial itself, through the grace of Christ, their character shines out in richer lustre and rarer splendor than ever in the days when their hearts were fullest of joy and gladness.

> "The night is mother of the day,
> The winter of the spring;
> And ever upon old decay
> The greenest mosses cling.
> Behind the cloud the starlight lurks;
> Through showers the sunbeams fall;
> For God, who loveth all his works,
> Hath left his hope with all."

So the life of the true home flows on, sometimes in the bright sunshine, sometimes in the deep shadow; yet whether in sunshine or in shadow it brings blessing. It shelters us in the day of storm. Its friendships remain true and loyal when adversity falls and other friendships are broken. It lays holy hands of benediction upon our heads as we go out to meet life's struggles and duties. Its sacred influences keep us from many a sin. Its memories are our richest inheritance. Its inspirations are the secret strength of our lives in days of toil and care. Then it teaches us to look toward heaven as the great Home in which all our hearts, hopes, and dreams shall be realized, and where the broken ties of earth shall be reunited.

RELIGION IN THE HOME

A German sculptor occupied eight years in making a marble statue of Christ. When he had wrought two years upon it, the work seemed to be finished. To test his success, he called a little child into his studio, and, showing her his statue, asked her, "Who is that?" She looked at it and replied, "A great man." The artist was discouraged. He had hoped that his conception of the Master had been so true that the pure eye of the child would recognize it at once. He began anew, and after a year or two more had passed, he invited the child again into his studio, and pointing to his new statue asked the same question as before: "Who is that?" She looked at it in silence for some time, a feeling of awe and reverence sweeping through her heart and expressing itself on her face until with eyes full of tears she said in low and gentle tones, "Suffer the little children to come unto Me." This time his work was not a failure. He had produced a figure in which the untaught instinct of the child saw the features of the Redeemer. His work had stood the severest test.

A somewhat similar test must be applied to all our

home-making. After we have done all in our power in building up a home, the husband his part, the wife hers, the parents theirs, the brothers and the sisters theirs, and when our home-life is full and complete, before we can say that we have realized the ideal of a true Christian home, we must prove its spirit. What impression would our home and its life make upon a pure and simple-hearted child?

We may build a palace of marble. We may fill it with the rarest beauties of art. We may adorn it in the most luxurious fashion. We may furnish it in the most costly manner. It may be perfect as a gem in all its appointments, a piece of art in itself. Then our home-life may be as stately as royalty itself. There may be the most perfect order, the loftiest courtesy, the utmost precision of movement. Each member of the family may fulfill his part with unfailing promptitude.

Bring in the child and ask it what it thinks of your home. "It is very beautiful," responds the little one. "It is very grand. It is a palace. Does a king live here?"

You turn away disappointed. You have failed to make such a home as you wished. You have piled up grandeur; you have made a splendid piece of art; you have succeeded in setting up a model which all will admire; but you have not made a home of love, of tenderness, and of praise.

You begin anew. You do not seek this time for grandeur. You build your home with taste and thought.

You put into it as many lovely things as you can afford. You set up your household life and fill it with the spirit of prayer, of love, of gentleness, of unselfishness. Again you call the child. She moves up and down, in and out. She sleeps under your roof; she eats at your table; she tastes of your pleasures; she mingles in the life of your household. You ask her what she thinks of your home, and she replies, "I think Jesus lives here!"

It is not the grandeur that impresses her now, but the spirit that dwells within; not the stateliness, but the affectionateness, not the courtliness, but the sweetness. She finds love every where—love that shows itself in tone, in act, in look, in word and in countless little manifestations of thoughtfulness and unselfish tenderness. It impresses the untaught feeling of the child as a home like that in which the Master would live.

This is the true test of home-making. It matters not how little or how much of grandeur, of luxury, of costly adornment there may be. Money and art can do many things, but they cannot make a home. There may be more of the spirit of a true home in a lowly cottage or in the one room where poverty finds a shelter, than in the stateliest mansion.

What is it that makes a home complete after all that the architect, the builder, the painter, the upholsterer, the furniture-maker and the decorator can do? What is it that comes into the furnished house and makes it a home? This is the question to which answer has been sought in all the former pages of this little book. The duties of the several members of the household have been considered. Suppose they all do their part with the highest fidelity possible in this world; what more is needed to complete the Ideal Christian Home? Is not the answer found in one word— God? If we leave him out, our most perfect home will be but like a marble statue with all the grace and beauty of life, but having neither breath nor heart-throb.

There are many reasons why religion is needed to complete the happiness and blessedness of a home. One is that nothing in this world is full and complete without the benediction of Heaven. "The blessing of the Lord, it maketh rich." All that labor and skill and soil and seeds can do for field or garden will not avail unless Heaven give rain and sunshine. Our very breath is God's gift, moment by moment. Our daily bread must come day by day from his hand. All our plans are dependent upon his prospering favor. Nothing can succeed without his approval and help. We are taught in the Scriptures to look to God for his blessing on every undertaking. The people were to bring the first sheaf of their harvest and the first ripe clusters from their vineyard to God's altar, before they had reaped a handful or gathered a grape for themselves, that his blessing might rest upon the whole harvest and vintage. They were to bring their children to God in the very opening of their

lives for consecration to him, that his blessing might rest
upon all their years. In the old patriarchal days, when the
tent was set up, if only for a night, an altar was also erected
and sacrifices of prayer and praise were offered to God.

We need the divine blessing on everything we have and
everything we do. Surely there is no work, no plan, no
undertaking in all the range of the possible things we may
do in the longest and busiest lifetime, on which we so much
desire God's benediction as upon our home. In nothing else
are so many sacred interests and such momentous
responsibilities involved. Nowhere else in life do we meet
such difficult and delicate duties. In nothing else is failure
so disastrous. A business venture may miscarry, and the
consequences will be much chagrin and disappointment,
some pecuniary loss, some hardship and suffering, but if
one's home is a failure, who call tell what wreck and sorrow
may result? If we need the divine blessing on some little
work of an hour, how much more do we need it in the
setting up of our home which carries in itself our own
happiness and the happiness of the hearts that are dearest to
us, and the eternal destinies of souls that shall creep into
our bosom and find shelter beneath our roof!

I have read that when the stones were all being carried
away, one by one, from an old ruin in Rome, thus
destroying one of the grandest relics of antiquity, the ruling
pontiff, to preserve it, set up a cross in the midst of it,

consecrating it by this act. It was thus made holy, and no one would touch it. The venerable pile was saved in this way from spoliation.

Every home in this world is exposed to a thousand dangers. Enemies seek to destroy it, to desecrate its holy beauty, and to carry away its sacred treasures. The very institution itself is assailed by the apostles of infidelity and licentiousness. Countless social influences tend to disintegrate the home, to rob it of its sanctities, to break down its sacred barriers, and to sully its purity. Nothing but the cross of Christ will save it. Those who are setting up a home, their hearts full of precious hopes of happiness and blessing, should consecrate it at once by erecting the altar of God in the midst of it. This will throw over it the protecting aegis of divine love.

We need religion in our homes to help us to do each his own part faithfully. Take the parents, for example—whose duties and responsibilities have been considered in a former chapter—into whose hands come tender young lives with infinite possibilities of development. They are to train these immortal souls into beauty and build up in them a noble manhood or womanhood. These lives are so sensitive that the slightest influences will leave imperishable impressions upon them, that a wrong touch may mar them for ever. They may have in them the elements of great power or usefulness; God may want them trained to be leaders in the world. For the upbuilding of their character, for the impressions that he stamped upon their souls, for their protection from unholy influences, for the moulding and shaping of their lives, for the development and training of their powers and for their preparation for life's mission and for eternity, the parents are responsible. Who is sufficient alone for these things? Where is the parent who feels ready in himself to assume all this responsibility—to take an infant child from God's hands to be tended, sheltered, taught, trained and led, and to answer at the end before God's bar for the faithful keeping of his sacred trust? Where is the parent who is prepared to engage to do all this and who wants no help from God? That so many do become fathers and mothers who never ask divine aid and wisdom only proves how thoughtlessly men and women can enter the most solemn mysteries of life, and with how little conception of their responsibility they accept the most momentous duties. Only the religion of Christ can fit parents for their high and holy responsibility.

We need religion in our homes in the time of sorrow. And where is the home into which sorrow comes not? We can build no walls strong enough or high enough to shut it out. We can gather within our doors no treasures so sacred that sorrow will never lay its hand upon them. Then when sorrow comes where shall we find comfort, if not in the religion of Jesus Christ? Shall we find anything in the splendors of architecture, in the beauties of art, in the luxuries of costly furnishing or adorning to bring calm and comfort to our hearts when one of our household lies in the struggle of death?

It is related of Heinrich Heine that he found himself in Paris during the scenes of the Revolution of 1848, in the very midst of the mad excitements. Weary, unbelieving, and almost hopeless in his endeavors to escape, he entered a room of the Louvre and fell down before that wonder of ancient art, the Venus di Milo. He looked up with almost worship of its divine beauty and with a vague desire for help as if this splendid figure could deliver him. But, though an object of exquisite beauty, its arms were broken off and it could not reach down to give him any aid. Its ears were marble and could not hear his cries. Its heart was stone and could not feel for him in his peril and alarm. So earthly grandeur and beauty all of us are to the human heart in its deep sorrow. A palace filled with rarest works of art can give no comfort to the stricken father and mother who, in one of its gilded and tapestried chambers, are sitting in anguish beside a dying child. I have seen such grief in the Christless, prayerless home, and pitiable indeed it was in its wild agony of despair. Though in the days of health and joy, no eye there was ever turned to God, no heart was ever lifted to him in praise or prayer, no voice ever cried to him for help or blessing; though religion was despised or ridiculed and there was no desire for God's minister within their doors, yet in the bitterness and hopelessness of their grief, when their refuge failed them, when only God could give help, they turned to him and begged for the ministry of religion. They wanted to hear the word of God read and prayer offered by the bed where the struggle with death was going on. There is something very sad in this despairing resort to the comforts of religion in the hour when all else has failed. Yet it ought to teach us the lesson that none but God will suffice in the time of great grief. Earth can build no home so beautiful, so perfect, that sorrow shall find there all it needs for comfort.

But in the home of prayer, when trial comes, there is help at hand. An unseen presence walks amid the shadows. A voice others hear not whispers peace. A hand others see not ministers consolation. Religion pours light in the darkness. The sorrow is no less bitter, but the stricken hearts are sustained in their pain or loss by the rich consolations of divine love. No home is prepared for the trials, which are at some time inevitable, which has not its altar standing in the centre whereon the fires burn perpetually.

Every home needs the *refuge* of religion. We live in a world of danger. Every life that grows up here must grow up amid countless perils. Human souls are delicate and tender. Our dear ones are exposed on every hand. Storms sweep the sea and the wreck goes down, burying noble lives beneath the waves; there is sorrow in homes when the missing ones come not. The battle rages on the bloody field and many a brave soldier falls to rise no more, or to rise scarred, maimed for life; there is grief in the homes where the cruel ball strikes. But there are fiercer storms raging in this world than those upon the sea, and our dear ones are exposed to them. There are more terrific battles on earth than those whose crash makes the mountains shake and which decide the fate of nations; and the tender souls of our households are in the very centre of the strife.

When our children go out from it in the morning to the day's duties, or in the evening to the night's scenes and pleasures, we know not to what terrible dangers they will be exposed before we see them again. We mourn for our dead, but if they have died in the arms of Christ they are safe. No danger ever can reach them. They have no more battles to fight. Do we never weep for our living when we remember to what perils they are exposed?

> "Lord, we can trust thee for our holy dead;
> They, underneath the shadow of thy tomb,
> Have entered into peace; with bended head
> We thank thee for their rest, and for our
>   lightened gloom."

"But, Lord, our living—who on stormy seas
Of sin and sorrow still are tempest-tossed!
Our dead have reached their haven, but for there—
Teach us to trust thee, Lord, for these, our
        loved and lost."

"For these we make our passion-prayer at night;
For these we cry to thee through the long day."

Yes, our dead in Christ are safe. They are folded away
under the shadow of God's wings.

"'What is death, father?'
'The rest, my child,
When the strife and toil are o'er;
The angel of God—who, calm and mild,
Says we need fight no more;
Who, driving away the demon band,
Bids the din of the battle cease,—
Takes banner and spear from our trembling hand,
And proclaims an eternal peace.'"

The children that we laid in Christ's arms in infancy, in
the sleep we call death, are forever safe. It is the living that
are in peril. It is life that is hard and full of danger; it is for
those living that we need to be anxious, lest they be

defeated in the field, where foes are thick and battles sore.

Where shall we find protection for these tender lives, save in the keeping of the almighty Saviour? We cannot shelter them ourselves. We cannot make our home doors strong enough to shield them. We cannot protect them even by love's tenderness or by the influence of beautiful things—of art, of luxury, of music, or by the refinements of the truest and best culture. From amid all these things children's souls are every day stolen away. All history and all experience proves that nothing but the religion of Christ can be a shelter for our loved ones from this world's dangers and temptations.

A friend was telling of a wonderful little flower which he discovered high up on the Rocky Mountains. In a deep fissure among the rocks, one midsummer day, he found the snow still lying unmelted, and on the surface of the snow he saw a lovely flower. When he looked closely, he perceived that it had a long, delicate stem, white as a tuberose, coming up through the deep snow from the soil in a crevice of the rock underneath. The little plant had grown up in spite of all obstacles, its tender stem unharmed by the cold drifts, until it blossomed out in loveliness above the snow. The secret was its root in the rich soil in the cleft of the rock, from which it drew such fullness of life that it rose through all to perfect beauty. A fit picture is that little flower of every tender child-life in this world. Over it are chilling masses of evil and destructive influences, and if it ever grows up into noble and lovely character, it must conquer its way by the force of its own inward life until it stands crowned with beauty with every obstacle beneath it. This it can do only through the power of the divine grace within. Its root must be honed in the sheltered warmth of piety, in the cleft of the Rock of Ages. Those who grow up in truly Christian homes, imbibing in their souls from infancy the very life of Christ, will be strong to overcome every obstacle and resist every temptation. The influence of godly example, the memories of the home altar, the abiding power of holy teachings, and the grace of God descending perpetually upon the young life in answer to believing prayer, give it such inspirations and impulses toward all that is noble and heavenly that it will stand at last crowned with honor and beauty. To make a home godless and prayerless is to send our children out to meet all the world's evil without either the shelter of covenant love to cover them in the storm or the strength of holy principle in their hearts to make them able to endure.

But what is it that makes a home a Christian home? What is home religion? These questions are important enough for most thoughtful consideration. Those who wish to cultivate flowers so as to bring out the richest possible beauty in them study long and diligently the nature of plant-life and the many conditions of soil, of temperature, of air and moisture essential to the growth of each particular kind of plant, and the development of each variety of flower, and then with scientific exactness produce in each case the right conditions. In our homes we are growing immortal lives. The problem is to bring out in each one the very highest possible development of manly or womanly character. There are certain conditions which are essential to all true growth. If men take such pains to know how to grow flowers which fade in a day, should we not take pains to know how to grow souls which live forever? What should be the religious atmosphere of a home to make it a true spiritual conservatory?

There must be a home altar. No Christian home-life can be complete where the family does not daily gather for worship. All the members may meet in God's house on the Sabbath for public service; each one may maintain strict habits of secret devotion; but if there is to be a family religion, a home-life blessed and sweetened by the grace of Christ, there must also be a family worship where all assemble to listen devoutly to God's word and bow reverently in supplication at God's feet.

There are many reasons why such worship should be observed. Shall we take all God's daily benefits from his hand and return to him no thanks? Shall we be dependent continually on his bountiful providence for food, for raiment, for protection, for love, and all the tender joys of home, and shall we never ask him for one of these blessings?

Shall we call our home a Christian home, and yet never worship Christ within our doors? Shall we call ourselves God's children, and yet never offer any praise to our Father? Should there not be some difference between a Christian and a heathen home? Should not God's children live differently from the children of this world? What mark is there that distinguishes our home from the home of our godless neighbor if there be no family altar?

There are many things that tend to cause friction in a household. There are daily cares. There are annoyances of a thousand kinds that break in upon the even flow of the family life. None of us are angels, and our intercourse together is ofttimes marred by selfishness or impatience or irritability or querulousness. Sometimes our quick lips speak the harsh word that gives pain to more than one tender heart in the household. We sometimes misunderstand each other, and a shadow hangs between two souls which love each other very truly. There is nothing that will smooth out all the little tangles and set all wrong things right again like the daily worship together. Every burden is there brought and laid off on the great Burden-bearer. Harsh feelings are softened as the admonitions of God's word fall on the ear. Hearts are drawn closer together as they approach the same throne of heavenly grace and feel the Spirit's power. Impatience vanishes from face and speech while all wait together before God. No bitterness against another member of the family can live through a tender season of household worship; while we plead with God to forgive our sins, we cannot but forgive one another. Peace comes to the perplexed soul while bowing at God's feet and feeling the great calm of his own peace brooding over us and lying all about us. We are ashamed of our disquiet and worry when we look up into our Father's face and see how faithfully he loves and cares for us.

"My mind was ruled with small cares to-day,
And I said pettish words, and did not keep
Long-suffering patience well; and now how deep
My trouble for this sin! In vain I weep
For foolish words I never can unsay.

"Yet not in vain, oh, surely not in vain!
This sorrow must compel me to take heed:
And surely I shall learn how much I need
Thy constant strength my own to supersede,
And all my thoughts to patience to constrain.

"Yes, I shall learn at last though I neglect
Day after day to seek my help from thee.
Oh, aid me, that I may always recollect

This gentle-heartedness and oh, correct
Whatever else of sin thou seest in me."

Bowing in prayer together in the morning strengthens all the household for life's activities. Wisdom is sought and obtained for the decisions and plans of the day. Guidance is asked and received. Help is drawn down from the throne of God. The children go out under sheltering wings and are safe in danger, guarded by angels and kept by Christ himself.

Thus reasons multiply why there should be family worship in every home. It is hard to see how any parent who realizes his responsibility can fail to have his household altar. Consider the matter frankly and honestly. You are a Christian man or a Christian woman. Your children look to you for the witness of Christ. What do they think of the absence of family prayer in their home? How does it impress them? Is your testimony before them what it should be? Can your religious life stamp itself on them if you never bow with them in prayer? Are you bringing to bear upon their tender lives all the hallowing influences needed to purify and keep pure the fountains of their hearts? You want their characters to be permeated with the truths of God's word. Can you hope that this will be so that they are not from childhood accustomed daily to hear these truths in their own homes? It is impossible to estimate full influence of the reading of the word in a home day after day and year after year. It filters into the hearts of the young. It is absorbed into their souls. It colors all their thoughts. It is wrought into the very fibre of their minds. It imbues them with its own spirit. Its holy teachings become the principles of their lives, which rule their conduct and shape all their actions.

Where every day the Bible is read in a home in the ears of the children, and its lessons simply and prayerfully taught, the effect is incalculable. It was thus that God himself commanded his ancient people to do—to teach the truths of his word diligently to their children when they sat in the house and when they walked by the way, when they rose up, and when they lay down. (Deut. ver. 6-9) This was the divine plan for bringing up a family—not a lesson now and then, but the incessant, uninterrupted, and continuous teaching of the Holy Scripture in the ears of the children. Such teaching unconsciously assimilates the character to the divine likeness. Even if there were no family prayer, the mere daily reading of the Scriptures year after year, continuously, would be in itself an inestimable influence for good. But where prayer is added, the household waiting together daily around God's feet, while heavenly gifts and favors are tenderly supplicated, who can sum up the total of blessing? What parent can afford to omit this duty and lose out of his home nurture this mighty element of power?

The excuses that are offered for the omission are

familiar. One pleads want of time. But he finds time for everything else that he really wants to do. Besides, time taken for duty is never lost. Will not the divine benediction on the day be worth more than the few moments of time it takes to invoke it? Then is there nothing worth living for in this world but business and money-making? Is the culture of one's home such a trivial matter that it must be neglected to get a few moments more each day for toiling and moiling in the fields of Mammon? Is the spiritual nurture of one's children so unimportant that it may with impunity be crowded out altogether to give one time to sleep a little later, or read the morning paper more leisurely, or chat with one's neighbors a few minutes longer? But honesty will compel men to confess that this excuse is never offered in sincerity.

Another pleads timidity. He cannot make a prayer in his family. He would break down. But is timidity a sufficient plea to excuse one from a duty so solemn, on which such vital interests of time and eternity depend? We had better test all our actions as we go on through life by inquiring how they will look at the judgment-day or from amid their own consequences at the end. When a parent stands at God's bar and this sin of omission is charged against him, will his answer, "I was too diffident," be sufficient to wipe out the charge? If his children, left unblessed in their tender years by the influence of household worship, grow up worldly and godless, drift away in sin and are lost, will it console the father and satisfy him, as he sits in the shadows of his old age and sees their ruin, to say "I was too timid"?

A Christian mother says that her husband is not a Christian, and that she has never had the courage to establish family worship. But many godly mothers have done so. There are mothers who every morning and every evening gather their children together to sing a hymn with them, read a chapter from God's word, and then bow in prayer invoking Heaven's grace upon their heads and upon the beloved father. It would be easy to cite examples proving the power of such hallowed faithfulness. It may at first be a cross for a mother to take up, but, like all crosses taken up for Christ's sake and for love's sake, the burden becomes a joy and an uplifting influence; out of the hard duty comes such blessing that the hardness is soon forgotten. There are men in heaven today or engaged now in earliest Christian service on the earth, because their godly wives had the courage to establish a family altar in the home. There are children all over the Christian world in whose hearts the sweetest memory of early years is that of the tender moments in the old home when they bowed in the daily prayer and the mother, with trembling tones, implored God's blessing upon her household.

"Little Willie Newton was a child about five years old. One day his mother had taken him into her room and prayed for him by name, and when she arose, he exclaimed, 'Mamma, mamma, I am glad you told Jesus my name; now he'll know me when I get to heaven. When the kind angels that carry little children to the Saviour take me and lay me in his arms, Jesus will look at me so pleased and say, "Why, this is little Willie Newton; his mother told me about him; how happy I am to see you, Willie!" Won't that be nice, mamma?"' Such links as this between a child's soul and heaven become in the end a chain of gold which no power can break.

It would be easy to add many other words to enforce and illustrate the importance of this duty. If these pages are read by parents who have no household altar, they are affectionately entreated, for the sake of their children, to set it up at once. It will bind the family more closely together. It will sweeten every joy and lighten every burden. It will brighten every path of toil and care. It will throw about the children a holy protection as they go out amid dangers. It will fill their hearts with the truths and influences of the divine word. It will weave into the memory of their home golden and silver threads which will remain bright for ever. It will keep continually open a way between the home and heaven, setting up a ladder from the hearthstone on earth to the Father's house in glory, on which the angels shall come and go continually in faithful ministry. Blessed is the home which has its family altar whose fires never go out.

But sad is the home, though it be filled with splendors and with the tenderness of human love, in which the household never gathers for united prayer.

It is very important that the family worship be conducted in such a way as to interest the younger members of the household, and even the little children. It ought to be made the brightest and most pleasant exercise of the day. In some instances, it is rendered irksome and wearisome. Long chapters are read, and read in a lifeless and unintelligible manner. The prayer is the same, day after day, a series of petitions of the most general kind, reaching out over all classes and conditions of men, except the little group that kneels about the altar, and embracing all the great needs and wants of the world, save the needs and wants of the family itself that bows together. If singing is part of the worship, the psalm or hymn is not carefully chosen for its appropriateness and fitness to the experiences and hearts of those who are to sing it. In the whole exercise, there is nothing to win the attention of the children or to interest them in the holy service. It is taken for granted that, because it is a religious act, it cannot be made pleasant and attractive; that children ought to sit still and listen attentively, even if the service is dull and wearisome; and that it is in evidence of their depravity that they fidget and wriggle on their chairs or carry on their sly mischief while the saintly father with closed eyes is droning over his stereotyped prayer.

But there is no reason in the world why religious exercises should be made dull and irksome. The family worship should be of such a character that it would be anticipated with eagerness, and that its memories would ever be among the most hallowed recollections of the childhood's home; each portion of the exercise should be enlivened by pleasing variety. Instead of being stately and formal, it should be made simple and familiar. Instead of requiring the children to listen in silence while the father goes through the whole worship alone, a part should be given to each member.

Just in what manner it is best to do this, each household must decide for itself. Indeed, no one method is always best, as variety is one of the elements of interest. In some families, the Scripture is read by verses in turn, every member reading. In others it is read responsively, the leader taking one verse and all the members together the next; in others the father alone reads. The matter of the selection of passages to read is important. Some heads of families follow the order of the Bible itself, going through it in course, not omitting a chapter or a verse. Many, in these later days, read the selection assigned for the next day of the meeting of the church. This is a good method, as it aids in the preparation of the lesson for the week, gathering the whole seven days reading and study around some one Scripture passage in which the children are for the time particularly interested.

An occasional topical lesson is pleasant and helpful. For instance, on Sabbath morning, let the reading consist of verses in brief passages from different parts of the Bible, all bearing upon the central topic of the day's lesson. On some day in the spring let all the verses that refer to flowers and plants be culled and read. When the first snow falls let all the passages that relate to snow be gathered from the Bible, with an appropriate word concerning each one. It will add to the interest in these exercises if the topic is announced in advance and each member of the family requested to find as many verses as possible bearing upon it. All Scripture-reading family worship will be brightened and its interest for children enhanced by an occasional explanatory remark or by all incident that illustrates the thought.

Singing should form part of the worship whenever possible. Occasionally—for instance, on the Sabbath evenings—it will be found profitable to hold a little family service of song, reading a verse or two of Scripture, and then singing a stanza of a psalm or hymn appropriate to the sentiment of the Bible passage.

The prayer in the household worship should be brief, particularly where the children are young. It should be fresh, free from all stereotyped phrases, couched in simple language that all can understand. It should be a prayer for the family at whose altar it is offered not altogether omitting outside interests, but certainly including the interests of the household itself. It should be tender and personal, freely taking up the members by name and carrying to the Lord the particular needs of each; remembering any who are sick, or in trouble, or exposed to danger or temptation. Some part in the prayer may also be given to the children. If the children are young they may repeat the entire prayer after the father, phrase by phrase. The Lord's Prayer may be used at the close, all uniting in it. In these ways the whole family will be interested in the worship, and it will become a delightful exercise, full of profit and instruction and rich with influences for good.

But family worship is not enough. There are homes where prayer is never omitted, yet in which there is not the spirit of Christ; *and only the spirit of Christ in a household makes a truly Christian home*. If the altar is in the midst, the whole life of the home should be filled with the incense that burns upon it. There are some fields of grass from which in summer days rises a sweet fragrance, although not a flower is anywhere to be seen. But when you part the tall grass and look down among its roots, there, close on the ground, hidden under the showy, waving grass, you see multitudes of small flowers, modest and lowly, yet pouring forth a delicate and delicious aroma filling all the air. There are homes in which there is nothing remarkable in the way of grandeur or elegance, yet the very atmosphere as you enter is filled with sweetness, like "the smell of a field which the

Lord hath blessed." It is the aroma of love, the love of Christ shed abroad in human hearts. Religion is lived there. The daily prayers bring down the spirit of Heaven. Christ dwells there, and his blessed influence fills with divine tenderness all the home-life.

It was said of one that "she looked like a prayer." If we would make our homes truly Christian homes, our daily lives must be like our daily prayers. If the members of the family wrangle and quarrel, the fact that the father is a minister or an elder, and the mother president of a Dorcas society or secretary of all association to send the gospel to China, does not make the home religious. If a blessing is asked at the table before the meal begins, and if then, instead of cheerful and affectionate conversation, the table-talk is made up of faultfinding with the food, of ill-tempered disputes amid acrimonious bickerings, the asking of a blessing surely does not make the intercourse Christian. If family worship is observed with scrupulous fidelity, and the members rise from their knees to violate the simplest lessons of Christian love and kindness in their fellowship as a household, the fact that there is family worship does not make a Christian home. The prayers must be lived. The Scripture lessons must find their way into the heart and then into the speech and conduct. The songs must sing themselves over and over all day in the household intercourse.

The lips that have breathed the sacred words of family prayer should never speak bitter, angry, or unkind words. A home in which the altar has been set up is thenceforth a consecrated spot. To surrender it to bickerings and strifes is sacrilege. It is holy unto the Lord, and should be a scene only of love and tenderness, of joy and peace.

It is said that in Greenland when a stranger knocks at the door, he asks, "Is God in this house?" If the answer is "Yes," he enters. So blessings and joys pause at our doors and knock to ask if God is in our dwelling. If he is, they enter; if he is not, they flee away, for they will not enter or tarry in a godless home. A young girl was engaged in a wealthy but prayerless household as a domestic servant. After spending one night under the roof, she came to her mistress pale and agitated and told her she could not stay with her any longer. When pressed for her reason she at length replied that she was afraid to live and sleep in a house in which there was no prayer. And there are no heavenly blessings that will enter or abide in a prayerless home. No divine guest is there. No wings of love droop down to cover the dwelling. It is a house without a roof, as it were, for it is written that God will pour out his fury upon the families that call not upon his name. But into the home where God abides, Heaven's richest blessings come, and come to stay. Angels encamp around it. It is roofed over with the wings of God. Its joys are all sweetened by the divine gladness. Its sorrows are all comforted by the divine sympathy. Its benediction rests upon all who go out from its doors. It is but the vestibule to Heaven itself.

There is no inheritance which the richest parent can bequeath to a child that can compare for one moment with the influence and blessing of a truly godly home. It gives to the whole trend of the life, away into the eternal years, such a direction and such an impulse that no after-influence, no false teachings, no terrific temptation, no darkening calamity, can ever altogether turn it away from its course. For a time it may be drawn aside by some mighty power of evil, but if the work in the home has been true and deep, permeating the whole nature, the deviation from rectitude will be but temporary. If parents give money to their children they may lose it in some of life's vicissitudes. If they bequeath to them a home of splendor, they may be driven out of it. If they pass down to them as a heritage only an honored name, they may sully it. But if they fill their hearts with the holy influences and memories of a happy Christian home no calamity, no great sorrow, no power of evil, no earthly loss, can ever rob them of their sacred possessions. The home songs will sing themselves out again in the years of toilsome duty. The home teachings will knit themselves into a fibre of character, rich in its manly or womanly beauty, and invulnerable as a coat of mail. The home prayers will bind the soul with gold chains, round the feet of God. Then, as the years go on and the old home of earth is broken up, it only moves from behind, as it were, and goes on before, where it draws the soul toward the better life.

For there is a home of which this earthly battle, even at its best, is but a type. Into that home God is gathering the great family. The Christian household that is broken here or scattered shall be reunited there. A father and his son were shipwrecked at sea. They clung to the rigging for a time and then the son was washed off. The father supposed he was lost. In the morning the father was rescued in an unconscious state, and after many hours awoke in a fisherman's hut, lying on a soft, warm bed. He turned his face, and there lay his son beside him on the same bed. So one by one our families are swept away in the sea of death. Our homes are emptied and our fondest ties are broken. But one in Christ Jesus we shall awake in the other world to see beside us again our loved ones whom we have lost here, yet who have only gone before us into the eternal home.

HOME MEMORIES

We are all making in our todays the memories of our tomorrows. Whether these shall be pleasant or painful to contemplate depends on whether we are living well or ill. Memory writes down everything where we shall be compelled to see it perpetually. There have been authors who, in their last days, would have given worlds to get back the words they had written. There have been men and women who would have given their right hands to blot out the memories of certain passages in their lives, certain acts done, certain words sent forth to scatter sin or sorrow.

"On the wall I see them, outlines vague and drear,
Strange, mysterious shadows, fraught with
        nameless fear,
Sometimes moving slowly, sometimes moving fast
Shadows from another world, shadows of the past;
Shadows faint, intangible—shadows, shadows all,
Yet my eyes discern them passing on the wall;

Sometimes moving slowly, sometimes moving fast,
Still their sad reflection o'er my soul they cast."

On the other hand, there are memories that shed a perpetual benediction. There have been artists whose eyes looked in old age upon the pictures they had painted, finding rare pleasure in the contemplation of the lovely things they had made; and there are hearts that are picture galleries filled with the memories of lives of sweetness, purity, and unselfishness. We are each preparing for ourselves the house our souls must live in the years to come. The poet Longfellow, in one of his tender poems, has these lines:

"Childhood is the bough where slumbered
Birds mid blossoms, many-numbered;
Age, that bough with snows encumbered.

Gather, then, each flower that grows
When the young heart o'erflows
To embalm that tent of snows."

The thought is very beautiful—that youth must gather the sweet things of life—the flowers, the fragrant odors, which lie everywhere, so that old age may be clothed with gladness. We do not realize how much the happiness of our after years will depend upon the things we are doing today. It is our own life that gives color to our skies and tone to the music that we hear in this world. The memories he makes along his years are the old man's heritage, his very home. He may change houses or neighbors or companions or circumstances, but he cannot get away from his own past. The song or the discord that rings in his ear—he may think it is made by other voices, but it is really the echo of his own yesterdays.

If you hold a polished shell to your ear, you shall hear as from within it a strange sound like the distant roar of the ocean. You even hear it said by people with fine imaginative powers, that this shell once lay by the shore of the sea, and that the sounds you hear as you hold it to your ear are the treasured echoes and old memories or the wild waves' thunder which it carries hidden in its recesses. But when you have made a few experiments with the shell, this pretty fancy vanishes. You lay it on a table and apply your ear, and then you do not hear the sound at all. It is only when you hold it in your hand that you hear the strange murmur. So the fact is learned that it is only the quivering of your own fingers, the throbbing of your own pulses against the hollow, resonant shell, that makes the sound. In like manner, the music which we hear as our years go on, whether it be sweet or discordant, is but the pulse-beat of our own hearts. We may think it comes from outside, and we may blame our circumstances if we are unhappy, but really it is the moan of the memories of our own past lives that saddens us.

What is true of our individual lives is true also of our homes. We are making their memories day by day and year by year, and what they shall be in the future will depend on the home-life we are living now. We may make our home a palace, filling it with delights covering the walls with beautiful pictures, planting flowers to fill the halls and chambers with fragrance, and hanging cages of singing birds everywhere to pour out sweet notes of song; or we may cover the walls with hideous images and ghastly spectres to look down upon us, and plant only briers and thorns about the doors to flaunt themselves in our faces when we sit in the gloom of life's nightfall. Or we may make the memories of our home so tender, so precious, so sacred, that each life that goes out of our doors shall carry a blessing upon it wherever it moves. Or we may make its memories a perpetual pillow of thorns for our heads, a burden of bitterness and anguish which shall never be lifted or removed.

There is no need for argument to prove the influence of the home memories in the formation of character. When one's childhood home has been true and sweet, its memories never can be effaced. Its teachings may long be unheeded and life may be a miserable waste. Sin may sweep over the soul like a devouring flame, leaving only blackened ruins. Sorrows may quench every joy and hope, and the life may be crushed and broken. But the memory of the early home lives on like a solitary star, burning in the gloom of night. Even in revels and carousels, its picture floats in the mind like a vanished dream. Its voices of love and prayer and song come back like melodies from some far-away island in the sea, when the lips that first breathed them out have long been silent in the grave.

There ought to be a powerful motive in this truth to lead us to watch the character of the memories we make in our homes. How will those who go out of our doors be affected in later life by what they remember of their early home? Will the memory be tender, restraining, refining and inspiring? Or will it be sad, bitter, and a curse?

Cowper's mother died when he was only six years old, yet so deep was the impression made upon him by her character that he said there was not a day in all his manhood's years when he did not remember and think of her. The memory of her tenderness hung over him like a soft summer sky. Will it be so with the children who are playing now in our homes? Is the mother who reads these words so impressing the tender lives of her children with the goodness of her own character that the memory and the influence shall remain when their hairs are white with awe and when she is long gone from earthly scenes?

There is a story of one who to his latest years was blessed by the memory of one incident in his childhood's home. When only a few years old, he was brought to his father's death-chamber to say good-bye to him. The godly man spoke a few words of wise, loving counsel to the boy, then drew him close to the bed, gave him a tender farewell kiss, and then, laying his trembling hand upon his child's head uttered a blessing, solemnly giving him to God. "Remember," said he, "that your dying father kissed you, blessed you, and gave you to God." All through his life, the memory of these solemn acts and words lingered with him. In his youth, when there came a temptation to do something wrong, the thought would flash: "No, I must not do this, for I am the boy that was kissed and blessed and given to God." This memory saved him many a time from yielding to sin. He must keep his soul clean because he had been given to God.

When, later in life, burdens pressed and sorrows weighed heavily, and he was about to give way to discouragement, to doubt or despair, again there would rise up before him the scene in that hallowed death-chamber, and the remembrance would sustain and support him: "I must not succumb to these sore trials. The Lord has not forsaken me. There must be something good yet to come out of all this darkness and bitterness. For am not I the boy that was kissed and blessed and given to God?" This memory was a star in the darkest midnights of his life, a morning star foretokening always the breaking of the day.

At last, in the sore stress of life's burdens, his mind gave way, and he spent several years in a hospital for the insane. Sometimes, in his brighter moments, he would speak as to his daughter in a strain like this: "Here I am shut away in this cheerless place, away from those I love. I am very lonely. I have no one now to play and sing for me as you used to do,

'Jesus lover of my soul,
Let me to thy bosom fly,'

or,

'Rock of Ages, cleft for me
Let me hide myself in thee.'

It all seems very dark and sad to me, and I cannot understand the mystery of this strange providence." Then there would break upon his mind again the dear, sacred old memory, and he would add: "Yet it must be right, for I am the boy that was kissed and blessed and given to God." Thus all through his years, through the darkest hours of his life, when every other bright thing seemed to have vanished, this hallowed memory remained a sacred benison to the latest moment.

One has written this testimony: "Many a night, as I remember lying quietly in the little upper chamber, before sleep came on, there would be a gentle footstep on the stair, the door would noiselessly open, and in a moment the well-known form softly gliding through the darkness would appear at my bedside. First, there would be a few pleasant inquiries of affection which gradually deepened into words of counsel. Then, kneeling her head close to mine, her most earnest hopes and desires would flow forth in prayer. How largely a mother can wish for her boy! Her tears bespoke the earnestness of her desire. I seem to feel them yet where sometimes they fell on my face. Rising, with a good-night kiss, she was gone. The prayers often passed out of thought in slumber, and came not to mind again for years, but they were not lost. They were safely kept in some secret place of memory, for they reappear with a beauty brighter than ever. I willingly believe they were an invisible bond with heaven that secretly preserved me while I moved carelessly amid numberless temptations and walked the brink of crime."

It would seem to be worthwhile for every mother to try to weave such memories into the early years of her children's lives. There is no surer way to bind them with chains of gold to God's throne. Where is the busy mother who cannot find time enough to spend thus a few moments every night with each child before it falls asleep, in sweet, loving talk and tender, earnest prayer? Far down into the years the memory of such sacred moments will go, proving thousands of times a light in darkness, an inspiration in discouragement, a secret of victory in struggle, a hand to restrain from sin in time of fierce temptation.

God has thus put into the hands of parents at their own hearthstone a power greater than that which kings and queens wield, and which must issue in either the weal or the woe of their children. It would surely seem to be worthwhile to make any sacrifice of personal comfort or pleasure to transmit a legacy of holy memories that shall be, through all the years, like a host of pure angels hovering over those we love, to guard and guide them.

There is one particular class of home memories of which a few words must be said. These are the memories we make in our intercourse one with another. Washington Irving wrote: "Ah! I go to the grave of buried love and meditate. There settle the account with thy conscience of every past endearment unregarded of that departed being who never, never can be soothed by contrition. If thou art a child, and hast ever added a sorrow to the soul or a furrow to the silvered brow of an affectionate parent; if thou art a husband, and hast ever caused the fond bosom that ventured its whole happiness in thy arms to doubt a moment of thy kindness or thy truth; if thou art a friend, and hast ever injured by thought, word or deed the spirit that generously confided in thee; if thou art a lover, and hast

ever given one unmerited pang to the true heart that now
lies cold beneath thy feet,—then be sure that every unkind
look, every ungenerous word, every ungentle action, will
come thronging back upon thy memory and knock
dolefully at thy soul; be sure that thou wilt lie down
sorrowing and repenting on the grave and utter the
unheard groan and pour the unavailing tear-bitter bemuse
unheard and unavailing."

The continual remembrance of this truth would
sweeten all our tones and give gentleness to all our actions
in our home intercourse. If we only could keep in mind all
the while how the memory of unkindness, bitterness, or
selfishness, one toward another, will pain our hearts when
one is taken and the other left, it would be one of the
mightiest of all motives for members of a family to dwell
together in unity.

A personal friend relates this incident: It was on a
bright winter morning that a young man, remarkable for
gentleness of manner and kindliness of heart, went out from
his father's house to his daily occupation. Within half an
hour, suddenly and without warning, he was called from
time to eternity; and before a third of the time he was
usually absent had passed, his lifeless form was carried into
the home he had left so happily a few hours before. Parents,
brothers, and sisters comforted each other as best they
could, but the sister nearest in age to the dead brother,

whose love and gentleness toward him none would question, seemed to have a sorrow peculiar to herself, which found vent to one who sought to comfort her in the bitter and regretful words, "I was not kind to him as he left home this morning."

No one ever knew to what she alluded. It may have been too keen a sense of delinquency which caused the bitter pain in her heart, or it may have been a playful word spoken, or perhaps the mere absence of the usual tenderness. With her loving nature and her unfailing gentleness toward this brother it could have been nothing really unkind. Yet it caused her sore pain as she looked upon the dead face. He could not hear her request now to forgive her, nor could any lavish tokens of love now atone for that which caused her pain. She had not been so kind as usual to him at parting that morning and the memory added much to the grief of her loving, tender heart over its sudden loss.

One bright summer morning a young man bade his wife and babe good-bye and went away to his work. Before midday there was an accident on the street; the scaffolding on which he was working gave way, and his lifeless body was carried back to his home from which only a few hours before he had gone out so happily. The news was broken as gently as possible; but there was one comfort that came with wondrous power to the crushed heart of the devoted young wife. The last hour they had spent in each other's company, in the morning, had been peculiarly happy, and their parting at the door had been unusually tender. She had not dreamed at the time that it would be their last talk together, yet there was not a word spoken which caused one painful memory now that she should never see him more nor speak with him again in this world. Every memory of that quiet talk at the breakfast table of the morning worship when they knelt side by side in prayer and of the tender good-bye on the doorstep was full of comfort. Through years of loneliness and widowhood the remembrance of that last hour has been an abiding source of gladness in her life, like a lamp of holy peace.

These two incidents illustrate the importance of unbroken tenderness and affectionateness in the family intercourse. In each moment of our home fellowship we are making memories which may become to us a source either of pleasure or of pain through long future years. We never can tell when we are having our last talk together, or our last meal, or when we are parting at the door never to meet again. Suppose, then, that as you go out in the morning you have a little strife or quarrel with one of the household whom you truly love, and you part, perhaps in anger, with sharp, stinging words, perhaps only in sullen silence. Do you not see how that parting may become a lifelong bitterness to you? Death may come to one of you to prevent your ever meeting again, and then the last memory will be one of pain. What a motive this should be to make the household intercourse tender and loving, without break or interruption, so that any word spoken, if it should prove to be the last, would leave a hallowed memory for the lonely years! Coventry Patmore's words are well worth remembering, applying them to our home friends:

"If thou dost bid thy friend farewell,
But for one night though that farewell may be,
Press thou his hand in thine.
How canst thou tell how far from thee
Fate or caprice may lead his steps ere that
    to-morrow comes?
Men have been known lightly to turn the
    corner of the street
And days have grown to months,
And months to lagging years, ere they
Have looked in loving eyes again."

    *   *   *   *

"Yea find thou always time to say some earnest word
Between the idle talk, lest with thee, henceforth,
Night and day, regret should walk."

So uncertain is life that any leavetaking may be forever. We are never sure that we shall have an opportunity to unsay the angry word and have it forgiven. The only safe way is to make every hour's fellowship in the household so sweet that if it should be the last it would leave a memory without regret.

There is another class of memories which, sooner or later, become part of the history of every home. These are memories of sorrows and losses.

"There is no flock, however watched and tended
But one dead lamb is there;
There is no fireside, howsoe'er defended,
But has one vacant chair.
"The air is full of farewells to the dying
And mournings for the dead."

There is no home into which grief does not come in some form. Nearly every house has its secret drawer, which is not very often opened, which contains the dresses, the tiny shoes, the dolls or toys of a little prattler whom God took.

"And oh, since that baby slept
So hushed, how the mother has kept,
With a tearful pleasure,
That little treasure,
And o'er it thought and wept
As it lies before her there
There babbles from chair to chair

A little sweet face
That's a gleam in the place,
With its little gold curls of hair."

Or perhaps it was not a child that died, but one who had lived to grow into all the life of the home and become its inspiration. The sorrow is not the same; the sense of loss is different. The longer we have had the loved ones in our clasp, the more is there to remember, the more touches are there left on the things about it to stir our hearts when we come upon them.

Or it may not have been in bereavement that the sorrow came. Ah! there are griefs worse than those which death causes. There are losses that leave a blacker blank than when the coffin-lid shuts down on the face and the grass grows green over the grave of one whom we shall see no more in this world.

It needs no skillful hand to touch and awaken the memories of sorrow in almost every home. Sometimes the whole household life has been changed into a tone of sadness by a grief bitterer than is common. Sometimes it has been a gentler stroke that has fallen, and the effect is only a deepening of seriousness and thoughtfulness, a softening of the tones of speech, a growing tenderness in all the intercourse. But sooner or later the music of every home must have its minor chords. There is a picture that is laid away. There is a vacant chair. There are mementoes of one who comes no more. There are songs that when sung choke every voice because they were favorites of one whose face is seen no more in the circle. There are books whose pages have a language for the heart not printed in words. There are places and scenes which bring it and a thousand sacred memories. Thus Whittier sings of the losses in the home:

"How strange it seems, with so much gone
Of life and love, to still live on!
Ah!, brother! only I and thou
Are left of all that circle now,
The dear home faces whereupon
That fitful firelight paled and shone
Henceforward, listen as we will,
The voices of that hearth are still;
Look where we may, the wide earth o'er,
Those lighted faces smile no more.
We tread the paths their feet have worn,
We sit beneath their orchard trees,
We hear, like them, the hum of bees
And rustle of the bladed corn;
We turn the pages that they read,
Their written words we linger o'er,
But in the sun they cast no shade,

No voice is heard, no sign is made,
No Step is on the conscious floor."

Such memories affect the home-life. They sober it,
sometimes sadden it. Sorrow is not always rightly borne.
Sometimes it puts out all the lights. But if it is endured in
the right spirit it leaves a blessing. Sorrow does not make
any true Christian home less tender. Rather it makes it all
the tenderer. Grief brings the members closer together.
We never love one another so much; we are never so gentle
toward one another, so thoughtful, so unselfish, as when a
common grief has touched us all. Indeed, sanctified sorrow
transfigures a home. It brings more of heaven down into it.
It sweeps away something of the earthliness that clings
always to unchastened love. It brings out many of the
better qualities of the household lives. It takes something
of the hardness out of every heart. It deepens the meaning
of life. If the music is not so loud afterward, yet it is
sweeter. If the joy is less boisterous, it is richer and fuller
after the grief has come.

"Heaven is not mounted to on wings of dreams,
Nor doth the unthankful happiness of youth
Aim thitherward, but floats from bloom to bloom,
With earth's warm patch of sunshine well content.

"Tis sorrow builds the shining ladder tip,
Whose golden rounds are our calamities,
Whereon, our firm feet planting nearer God
The spirit climbs and hath its eyes unsealed.

     *   *   *   *

"Through the clouded glass
Of our own bitter tears we learn to look
Undazzled on the kindness of God's face;
Earth is too dark, and heaven alone shines through."

It may truly be said that no home ever reaches its highest blessedness and sweetness of love and its richest fullness of joy till sorrow enters its life in some way. The best home music can be brought out only in the fire of trial. Did you ever sit on a winter's evening before an old-fashioned open fire place with its andirons and its blazing log of wood?

As you sit there and watch the fire playing about the log you begin to hear a soft sound, a clear musical note perhaps, or a tender quavering strain, plaintive and sad. It takes every tone as the evening passes. Sometimes it sounds like a whole chorus of bird-songs; sometimes it dies away into a faint murmur. What is it? Are there birds hidden in the chimney that give out these strange notes? Are there invisible spirits hovering about the room, that breathe out these plaintive strains? No, the music comes from the log in the fire. The flames bring it out. If you are of a poetical turn of mind you will imagine that long ago in the forest the birds sat on the branches of the tree from which this back-log was taken, and sang there, and their songs hid away in the wood, where they have remained ever since. Or you will fancy that the winds sighed and murmured through the branches in gentle summer breezes, or swept through them in furious storms, and that the music of the breezes or of the storms has been imprisoned in the heart of the tree all these many years. And now in the hot flames all this long-slumbering music is brought out.

This may be but a pretty poetic fancy, so far as the weird music of the log on the hearth is concerned, but it is no mere fancy that the sweetest, fullest music of the home is not drawn out until the fires of trial come. The bird-notes of joy that warble about the ears in the sunny days of childhood and youth sink away into the heart and hide there. The lessons, the influences, the gladness, the peace of quiet prosperous days seem to have been lost. The life does not appear to yield its true measure of joyfulness. Then the fires of trial kindle about it, and in the flames the long-gathering and imprisoned music is set free and flows out. We all know lives of which this is the true history. The world's richest songs have been sung in the midst of the hot fires. What is true of individual life is true also of household life. Our love for one another may be true and deep in the sunny days, but it never reaches its richest development until pain or suffering touches us and calls out all the hidden wealth of affection. The mother's love for her child, rich and deep as it is, never attains its full wondrousness of self-denial and sacrifice until the child is sick or in some pain and the mother bends over it in yearning solicitude and unselfish ministry. The same is true of all the home affections. It is the fire that brings out the imprisoned music. The household that has endured sorrow in the true spirit of faith and resignation comes out of it with richer and tenderer love. Husband and wife that bend side by side over a dead child are drawn to each other as never before. The other children are dearer to the parents after one has been taken. Brothers and sisters grow more patient and thoughtful toward one another when their circle has been broken. An empty chair has a wonderful power to soften home hearts and refine the feelings of nature.

Thus the memories of grief and trial in a truly Christian home are not discordant notes in the song, but become really its sweetest voices. As the years come and go the remembrance of losses and disappointments loses its bitterness and becomes a source of joy rather than of pain. Jean Ingelow writes:

"Sorrows humanize our race;
Tears are the showers that fertilize the world;

And memory of things precious keepeth warm
The heart that once did hold them.

"They are poor
That have lost nothing they are poorer far
Who, losing, have forgotten; they most poor
Of all who lose and wish they might forget
For life is one, and in its warp and woof
There runs a thread of gold that glitters fair,
And sometimes in the pattern shows most sweet
Where there are sombre colors.

"Let us turn
Oft and look back upon the wondrous web,
And when it shineth sometimes we shall know
That memory is possession."

So it ofttimes comes that the very tenderest and richest memories of a home are the memories of its sorrows. They are golden chains that bind hearts together in tenderest clasp. Then when Christian faith rules in the heart the mementoes of grief and loss become inspirers of new hopes. We are richer for having loved although we have lost. Tennyson in "In Memoriam," says:

"This truth came borne with bier and pall—
I felt it when I sorrowed most
'Tis better to have loved and lost,
Than never to have loved at all."

We are richer also for having suffered if we have suffered with resignation and trust in God. Then we are richer also in immortal possessions. Our dead are not lost to us; they have only passed into a higher, fuller, safer life, where they are secure for ever from danger and trial, and secure also for us. As Whittier writes again:

"And yet, dear heart I remembering thee,
Am I not richer than of old?
Safe in thy immortality,
What change can reach the wealth I hold?
What chance can mar the pearl and gold
Thy love hath left in trust for me?
And while in life's late afternoon,
Where cool and long the shadows grow,
I walk to meet the night that soon
Shall shape and shadow overflow,
I cannot feel that thou art far,
Since near at need the angels are;
And when the sunset gates unbar
Shall I not see thee waiting stand,

And, white against the evening star,
The welcome of thy beckoning hand?"

And again the same gentle poet writes:

"Yet Love will dream, and Faith will trust
(Since He who knows our need is just),
That somehow, somewhere, meet we must.
Alas for him who never sees
The stars shine through his cypress trees I
Who hopeless lays his dead away,
Nor looks to see the breaking day
Across the mournful marbles play
Who hath not learned, in hours of faith,
The truth to flesh and sense unknown,
That Life is ever Lord of Death,
And Love can never lose its own!"

It is not every home whose memories are such a heritage of blessing. An ungodly home twines about the tender lives of the young no such sacred cords to bind them to truth, to virtue, and to love. The intercourse of an unloving household leaves no such joy-fountains in the hearts of its members. In a Christless, prayerless home sorrows are not thus transfigured and changed into blessings. It is only where Christ is a guest that the home-life is so enriched and illumined. It is only his presence that will sanctify every influence and hallow every memory.

It has been pointed out that the upper half of the panels in our common doors represents the cross. If the panels are taken out the cross appears in true and exact proportions. Many persons may have noticed this, but not many know perhaps that this form was purposely adopted in the Middle Ages, and that it is no mere accident of architecture. Dr. Phelps, speaking of this, says: "It was no fortuitous circumstance or geometric convenience in domestic building. It had its origin in the religious fervor of the Crusades, which made everything that could be thus employed an emblem of the central truths and forms of Christian worship. The same religious tastes which constructed the ancient cathedrals in the form of the cross, and scattered crosses and the instruments of our Lord's passion everywhere by the roadside, gave structure to windows and doors. Windows in mediaeval castles, and in the upper class of humbler homes as well, were divided by the Roman cross, the pillar running perpendicularly through the centre and the cross-beam near the top; so that every eye that looked out upon the outside world should look through the type of the central thought of the Christian faith. . . . With the same design the paneling of doors was so constructed as to form the same device.

"From that day to this, this usage of household

architecture has remained—a silent witness to the devotion of another age. To mediaeval piety it must have been an impressive circumstance of daily life that every time one passed through a doorway one faced the emblem of the great Christian tragedy. Entering the room where the daily meals were served, or going to the chamber of repose at night, every inmate of the home looked upon the sign of the sacrifice on which the salvation of all depended and the same token was one of the first images to greet the eye in the morning. The Christian home, however lowly, if it rose to the dignity of paneled doors and windows, was thus crowded with reproductions of the symbol which the sensitive religious temperament of the age made sacred to all, and which often brought tears to the eyes of many. By such expedients did our fathers strive to make the great thoughts of the Christian faith a pervasive presence with themselves and their children."

It can do us no harm in these later days to recall and keep in mind the mediaeval piety which sought thus to place a memorial of Christ at the entrance to every room, building into every part of the very house itself the symbol of his great love. The form itself is nothing. It wards off no evil. It brings no blessing to a home. But if the symbol suggest thoughts of Christ and his love and holiness whenever the eye rests upon it, its influence must be to soften the heart, to check and restrain evil words and tempers, to kindle the spirit of devotion and to sweeten all the life of the home. Anything that helps to keep us in mind of the presence of Christ and of his loving spirit cannot do us harm.

But far more important is it for us to make sure that we have Christ himself in our home. Symbols are nothing unless they are the true pictures of sacred facts. If Christ be indeed remembered daily and hourly in the home, if his presence be consciously realized and its transforming power felt in each heart, and if everything be done and every word spoken in his name, the household life will be pervaded by the spirit of heaven, and the home memories will be tender with all the hallowed tenderness of the warmest love.

We are fast moving on through this world. Soon all that will remain of us will be the memories of our lives. No part of our work will then afford such a true test of our living as the memorials we leave behind us in our homes. No other work that God gives any of us to do is so important, so sacred, so far-reaching in its influence, so delicate and easily marred as our home-making. This is the work of all our life that is most divine. The carpenter works in wood, the mason works in stone, the smith works in iron, the artist works on canvas, but the home-maker works on immortal lives. The wood or the stone or the iron or the canvas may be marred, and it will not matter greatly in fifty years; but let a tender human soul be marred in its early training, and ages hence the effects will still be seen. Whatever else we slight, let it never be our home-making. If we do nothing else well in this world, let us at least build well within our own doors.

The last song and the most beautiful that Mozart sang was his Requiem. He had been engaged upon this exquisite piece for several weeks, his soul filled with inspirations of richest melody. After giving the last touch, and breathing into it that undying spirit of song which was to consecrate it for all time, he fell into a gentle and quiet slumber. At length the light footsteps of his daughter awoke him.

"Come hither, my Emilie," he said; "my task is done. The Requiem, my requiem is finished."

"Say not so, dear father," spoke the gentle girl; "you must be better; even now your cheek has a glow upon it."

"Do not deceive yourself, my child," said the dying father; "this wasted form can never be restored by human aid. Take these, my last notes; sit down by my piano here and sing them with the hymns of thy sainted mother. Let me once more hear those tones which have so long been my solace and delight."

Emilie obeyed, with a voice enriched by the tenderest emotion. Then, turning from the piano when she had finished she looked in silence for the approving smile of her father, but there wait instead only the still, passionless smile which the rapt spirit had left, with the seat of death upon his features. He had gone home on the wings of his own Requiem.

There is no requiem so sweet for the departing spirit as the hallowed memories of a true home. They will make music in the heart in its last moment inspiring as the songs of angels.

May God help every one of us to live at home so tenderly, so unselfishly, so lovingly, that the memories we make within our own doors shall be our own holiest requiem, on the breath of which our spirits may be wafted away to glory in the Home in our Father's House!

THE END.